KNEE TO KNEE,
EYE TO EYE

KNEE TO KNEE, EYE TO EYE

Circling In on Comprehension

ARDITH DAVIS COLE

HEINEMANN
PORTSMOUTH, NH

Heinemann
A division of Reed Elsevier Inc.
361 Hanover Street
Portsmouth, NH 03801-3912
www.heinemann.com

Offices and agents throughout the world

The author and publisher wish to thank those who have generously given permission to reprint borrowed material:

Reviews of *The Search for Delicious, The Breadwinner, The Mozart Season*, and *Juniper* are reprinted by permission of Chinaberry Inc. Copyright © 2002 by Chinaberry Inc.

Library of Congress Cataloging-in-Publication Data
Cole, Ardith Davis.
    Knee to knee, eye to eye : circling in on comprehension / Ardith Davis Cole.
        p. cm.
    Includes bibliographical references.
    ISBN 0-325-00494-3 (alk. paper)
    1. Literature—Study and teaching (Elementary).   2. Group reading.   3. Children—Books and reading.   I. Title.

LB1575.C64 2003
372.47—dc21   2002155230

Editor: Lois Bridges
Production: Vicki Kasabian
Cover design: Jenny Jensen Greenleaf
Typesetter: Publishers' Design and Production Services, Inc.
Manufacturing: Steve Bernier

Printed in the United States of America on acid-free paper
07 06 05   RRD   4 5

This book is dedicated to

the memory of my mom,
Lillian Davis,
who shared with all of us
the beauty inherent in real-life,
knee-to-knee, eye-to-eye conversations

and to

all the Erics of this world
who internalize and then act on
the meanings that rich conversations evoke.
They are the hope for our future.

CONTENTS

Infinite Story

Story:
The celebration of life
The substance of man's ongoing drama,
The essence of who we are.
From a baby's first breath
story emerges.
It is the patchwork sewn
by the threads of our lifeblood.
Our days are choreographed upon its pages.
We arise each morning
to the story of that day—
happy or sad,
exciting or dull,
we sculpt our way
creating each day's
unique
yet similar
stories:
morning stories of
our spouse,
child;
school stories of
our friends,
colleagues,
students,
authors;
evening stories of
our families,
clubs,
newspapers,
televisions,
books.
Even as we sleep
story finds its roots
in the deepest recesses of who we are:
Story!
Infinitely
Man's Gift to Man
God's Gift to Humanity.

Ardith Davis Cole
(1989)

ACKNOWLEDGMENTS

In conversation, we practice good human behaviors. We think, we laugh, we cry, we tell stories of our day. We become visible to one another. We gain insights and new understandings.
Margaret Wheatley, Turning to One Another (2002, 140)

This book gathered its basic insights and understandings in the '80s when my Lockport, New York, primary classes and I struggled to create conversations that looked and felt real. I therefore first thank my students—especially those who presented a literature conversation ten years ago at the Whole Language Umbrella conference in Niagara Falls: Eric, Chrystal, Jessica, Lindsay, Zach, Michael, Sarah, Jennifer, Fallon, Joey, Kyla. You gave me the faith.

Then, chapters were refined and extended while I was a K–12 language arts specialist in Sweet Home district in Amherst, New York. It was then I came to understand that the model could work for all elementary teachers. I feel especially indebted to K–5 colleagues at Maplemere, who put up with my shenanigans for nine years. They are such a wonderful group of dedicated, constructivist teachers who follow both their learned minds and their compassionate hearts while deciding what's best for kids. Again and again, their names grace the pages of this book. Their generosity remains ongoing. Plus, I was blessed with supportive administrators, such as Superintendent Dr. Gary Cooper and Maplemere principals Dr. Michelle Kavanaugh and Ann Laudisio. I truly thank all of my Sweet Home colleagues for their ideas, patience, generosity, and professionalism. Without them I doubt I would be sitting here finishing this book.

To all those in Buffalo City Schools, whose classrooms and kindnesses have been shared with me over the past two years, I say thank you so much—especially to the fourth grades at School 45. Denise Vassar even visited students' homes during the summer, collecting the missing permission signatures.

I am indebted to all those colleagues with the Board of Cooperative Education Services, Western New York school districts, Niagara Frontier Reading Council, New York State Reading Association, International Reading Association, National

Council of Teachers of English, University of Buffalo, and Buffalo State College who, throughout the past fifteen years, invited me to present this conversation model to their constituencies. Our discussions helped sculpt meanings, and together, we all grew.

Furthermore, there are authors whose ideas helped shape this book. I sincerely thank Frank Smith, who understands literacy better than anyone else I know; Stephanie Harvey and Ann Goudvis, who gave the profession some solid substance for the teaching of comprehension in *Strategies That Work*; Margaret Wheatley, whose book *Turning to One Another* is a blueprint for humanity; and the Chinaberry people for their kind generosity in allowing the use of their online reviews.

Of course I thank my friends and family for their ongoing love and support related to all the urgencies and burdens that writing demands. I offer a very special thank-you to my grandchildren, Cameron and Delanie, who assisted me in a variety of book-related tasks; to Carolyn and Marly, who patiently retrieved East Coast information for me (on the West Coast); and to Elaine, who has encouraged this endeavor from the time she was part of our classroom community.

Last, but certainly not least, I thank Heinemann for believing in this work. I am especially grateful to my kind and caring friend and editor, Lois Bridges, who always knows just what to say to make one's day a little better. Her assistant, Karen Clausen, was helpful and patient, gathering all pieces into a final form. I also sincerely appreciate the care and concern given by production editor Vicki Kasabian. I hope I remember all the writing lessons I learned from these wonderful "teachers."

And, of course, I thank you, the reader, for investing your time, effort, and money in my ideas. I promise you, they work.

INTRODUCTION

"Like we did with the slaves? That was awful!"

"Yeah, I wouldn't want that to happen to me."

"Me neither."

"How would it feel if people came to our houses and started burning down our houses and—"

"In our back yards—"

"And started beating up on people?"

"Yeah, you gotta think of yourself, too."

"You gotta think of like, what could happen if sometime they turn back on you? And they started doing the stuff that you were doing to them?"

"Like those people said, 'You can't be friends with somebody who makes fun of somebody, cause then they're gonna end up making fun of you.'"

Transcribed from Kirsten Baetzhold's
third graders' response to Roll of Thunder, Hear My Cry

Children reading for real reasons—digging to the depths of meaning and captured by the experience! Kids helping each other construct a kinder, gentler world. This is what literature conversations are all about.

I am committed to literature conversations because I have watched them change lives and perspectives. I've seen them build confidence and compassion. I truly believe that if all teachers committed to the conversation process, it would change the way in which students interact, both in and out of the classroom. Indeed, literature conversations can produce dramatic consequences—and not just socially and emotionally, but intellectually, as well.

WHY TEACHERS?

Why should educators have to worry about teaching students how to orally converse on a given topic? We should because talking helps students clarify and organize their thoughts. We should because it helps them solve problems, revise their thinking, and connect to other situations, people, and events, but also because children learn how to belong and how to get along.

Furthermore, literature conversations provide a platform for deep, rich comprehension of text. By developing these classroom structures for talk, teachers can help students collaborate, substantiate their ideas, and negotiate. Unfortunately, I hear many teachers say, "I don't have time to do literature conversations, because we have more important things to do."

LITERATURE CONVERSATIONS:
A CONTEXT FOR INTELLECTUAL GROWTH

Guided Comprehension Perks

Some people think of literature conversations as fluff. Not so! The intellectual perks are extraordinary. First of all, students acquire a richer, deeper meaning of text. This book will show how they crawl between the lines and dredge out inferences and innuendoes, how they take a stand and support it with textual evidence, and how they make connections to their own lives, other texts, and the craft of the author. Furthermore, kids become turned on to reading and make it an integral part of their lives. Thus, fluency grows while reading rate and vocabulary are enhanced.

The lowest level of questioning and its related responses (those concerned with facts, knowledge, literal comprehension, or content) can be evaluated on a multiple-choice test. But if we focus only on these, we neglect the higher levels of thinking. We need to change the present school culture of regurgitation into a mindful, creative one where higher levels of thinking (related to application of facts, analysis, synthesis, and evaluation) move readers into constructing their own knowledge. That is what the examples in this book will demonstrate, and I invite you to dive into the guided comprehension protocol through them.

Using *guided comprehension*, *Knee to Knee, Eye to Eye* demonstrates how students learn through their teacher's modeling of strategies. A variety of conversation structures will help kids learn the basics in comprehension: how to question, predict, make connections, infer, determine importance, evaluate, and synthesize. These strategies are what research says comprehension is all about (Harvey and Goudvis 2000; Pressley 2000; Burns, Griffin, and Snow 1999; Beck et al. 1997; Cunningham and Allington 1994; Weaver 1988; Anderson et al. 1985).

Speaking Perks

Certainly, if literature conversations promote higher-level thinking, they should be places of rich discussion—and indeed, they are! Maybe that is why some of the world's greatest intellectual leaders were a part of conversation groups known as *salons*. "Originally devoted to art and literature, the salon was so diverse that topics soon included science and politics" (Sandra and Spayde 2001, 16). Exactly who were these intellectuals who belonged to talk communities? People like Rene Descartes, Aldous Huxley, D. H. Lawrence, Pablo Picasso, Albert Einstein, Sigmund Freud, Gertrude Stein, Carl Rogers, Edna Ferber, and, of course, Bill Moyers. Some of these individuals actually interacted in the same salon!

Maybe that is why one of this country's most prestigious private schools, Phillips Exeter, borrowed Martin Luther's "table talk" structure to teach *all* of its classes. Some educators say (Manzo 2002) that only students such as those at Exeter can effectively use their Harkness roundtable method. However, I know better. I know that conversation works for high-poverty schools, too. As a matter of fact, that is where I first developed the steps for the process I share in this book. And, it is in such schools that I continue to nurture the seeds of conversation.

Sandra and Spayde (2001), who have studied conversation communities, tell us that the art of conversation is governed by two areas of communication: speech and silence. These authors suggest nine touchstones to a good conversation: brevity, clarity, specificity, originality, tact, sincerity, lightheartedness (wit and humor), argument, and active listening. When we offer classroom experiences in these areas, we are truly helping kids learn how to "win friends and influence people," for these are not only keys to successful school learning but also keys to living a rich, full, rewarding life.

Social Perks

The intellectual payoffs are not the only perks. Literature conversations also have a positive influence on social interaction, relationships, and community spirit.

Again and again, I see wonderful things happen in classrooms that offer students shared voice venues. I believe that without such collaborative talk experiences, our country will continue to experience conflict and violence. Others who have researched such contexts would no doubt agree (Kohn 1996; Johnson and Johnson 1995; Clarke and Mills 1979; DeCecco and Richards 1974; Deutsch 1973).

I like the way Sandra and Spayde (2001) explain the social-emotional consequences of such regular talk groups:

> Shared time ensures shared experiences, which in turn foster emotional links between people. When people spend enough time with others in a common endeavor, they grow to love and care about them—even if they don't see them socially or count them as close friends. (177)

Our kids need these mini talk groups as much socially and emotionally as intellectually. They need them for the community they offer, because involvement in a safe and caring group of people is a missing ingredient in the lives of many.

LITERATURE CONVERSATIONS: A CONTEXT FOR COMMUNITY SPIRIT

What Is a Community?

Award-winning writer and consultant for both schools and corporations, Margaret Wheatley laments today's social isolationism:

> For as long as we've been around as humans, as wandering bands of nomads or cave dwellers, we have sat together and shared experiences . . . but today we are alone. We are more fragmented and isolated from one another than ever before. (2002, 4)

However, literature conversations help heal this sense of isolation by creating community. They are places of inclusion; that is, members search for reasons to invite people in, rather than to keep people out. As a matter of fact, "In community, instead of being ignored, denied, hidden, or changed, human differences are celebrated as gifts" (Peck 1987, 62). Through the processes and products related to literature conversations, classrooms become that kind of vibrant, transactive, collaborative environment. And, at this moment in history, our children are greatly in need of the support and motivation a true community will offer.

The Bad News
A lack of human connections
This new century finds us in a far different environment from the last, for ours is no longer an agrarian economy. Today, western society claims a soil that lies fallow in want of rich conversation and true community. We are now able to satisfy

our seeming needs exclusively, that is, without exchanging words with another human being. We can be entertained by an electric screen of one sort or another. We can have our appetites satiated, our thirsts quenched, our cars washed, and our newspapers purchased by merely depositing money into a machine. Public transportation allows us to purchase tickets from metal boxes (or strangers) and then hurriedly slip our headphones on or launch our laptops into action, as we allow a vehicle to move us between home and work. We, who are ushering in this new century, now fill our days with effective efficiency, but rarely do any of us enter into meaningful, committed conversation. Think about it.

And what of our children in this new century? They awaken at about the same time they did one hundred years ago, but now they watch television before they put a frozen waffle in the toaster and board the school bus—usually a place of shouting, not talk.

According to many, however, school is still one place that has not changed much in the past century. A short jaunt down most school hallways will demonstrate that it is teachers' voices that predominate. Furthermore, when today's youngsters arrive home after school, they often head straight for their Gameboys, Segas, or a TV program filled with questionable morals and violence. Some partake of sports, but these are organized activities—places of competition, not cooperative conversation.

Where can today's kids learn to navigate a human relationship with grace and finesse? Where can they learn to work out problems in a civil manner? To support others by acting interdependently? To understand another's point of view? Where in this world can they do that? At school? At home?

A viewing culture

In Bhutan, where modern technology is a rare commodity, family conversations abound (D'Aluisio and Menzel 1996). However, in the United States, a major part of a student's out-of-school life is spent in front of a television. What are kids learning from all those hours of TV? The answer to that question can be found in a number of places. First of all, we can turn on CNN or the local news and listen for a few minutes. We'll of course first hear the latest celebrity saga. But, if we listen a bit longer, we will hear of the numerous protestations, confrontations, and altercations, within families, between races, and amongst countries. It becomes apparent that at a number of levels we have communication deficiencies and, thus, relationship problems. This is what our young people are learning. It is obvious that television is not the place to build relationships and grow communities. Actually, it is probably exacerbating their demise.

Children are learning that we don't get along with each other very well, which is also evidenced by divorce and suicide rates, student conflicts, and every kind of abuse. As a matter of fact, kids have learned this so well that two-thirds of today's teens worry about being harmed by violence while they attend school (Schaps, Schaeffer, and McDonnell 2001). This is definitely not good news. Let us turn then, instead, to some good news.

The Good News

I see the good news unfolding in our classrooms, because they are the places where we teachers can make a difference—a difference in students' academic abilities, but also in their social and emotional development. We cannot solve all the problems in this world, but we can surely work toward solving some.

Good news in the academic areas

In this, the day and age of written performance tests, certainly literature conversations become a needed rehearsal for students' written responses. That is, they lay the foundational skills and the confidence for the entire response process. Thus, through oral response experiences, we see written response improve, and along with it, students' performance on related assessments. Why not, then, enhance written performance through its rehearsal in literature conversations?

We can also make a difference in the area of text comprehension. That is, teachers who use the guided comprehension protocols in this book will enhance student comprehension overall—and not just during literature conversations. As kids are motivated to substantiate, validate, investigate, and evaluate their responses for book talks, they are internalizing a real-life process that will be carried across the curriculum. So let's begin.

Good news in the social-emotional areas

It is primarily through our relationships with others that we can grow, both as individuals and as a society. Meg Wheatley (2002) tells us: "Relationships are all there is. Everything in the universe only exists because it is in relationship to everything else. Nothing exists in isolation" (19).

Yet today's competitive culture often sees relationships as ends in themselves, ones in which individuals follow an I-win-you-lose mentality. "Many of us have been rewarded for these [competitive] behaviors. We've become powerful through their use. But none of these lead to wise thinking or healthy relationships" (Wheatley 2002, 32). They harm not only relationships but also community spirit. This does not have to be. We do have a choice.

If we help kids learn how to change "Here's what I want" to "How can I help," we turn a win-lose competitive situation into a win-win collaborative celebration. So let's do it!

An ancient truth explains that if we teach a child values at an early age, when he grows up he will follow those values. It is not surprising, then, that when the National Institute of Mental Health documented the development of empathy and altruism in children, they found that "the capacity of young children to reach out to others in need is shaped by their socialization" (Holland 1998, 29). Some say there is a critically receptive period in the brain's development when empathy should be taught, or it may never fully awaken (Maclean 1995). Therefore, if our students do not experience democratic and moral values in their home lives, we teachers have an obligation to them and to our society to create opportunities where feelings such as empathy and compassion may arise. It seems that good books and rich conversations, rather than lectures, would be the key to such possibilities. So let's do it.

We know that when individuals feel like they have some control over their learning they invest more. They make choices directed toward their interests and, as a consequence, develop greater skill in those areas. That is why we have young experts in almost everything from golf to chess. Certainly, literature conversations allow choices to occur and interests to flourish—especially now that we have millions of wonderful text options lying at our doorsteps. So let's start!

LITERATURE CONVERSATIONS: DEMOCRACY IN TRAINING

Can one teacher actually change the tides of culture? Only if she is willing to commit to *truly* restructuring the classroom environment so that it becomes a place where individuals learn how to transact with, care for, and care about others. The final result is an interdependent community—that is, a democracy. Such a teacher commitment will be rewarded again and again as the structure becomes internalized and the content drives the process.

The Structure of a Literature Conversation

Literature conversations take place between and among individuals who sit within an eye-to-eye structure to talk about what they have read or heard. That is, they take place between partners or within student circles, where members are free to talk about what was heard or read. They are a dialogue.

Literature conversations differ from real-life conversations in that these book talks have an anchor, the text. Real-life conversations may flow from the day's weather to a sick aunt to the new supermarket, whereas literature conversations, by their very nature, require students to stay connected in some way to the text.

Such a community of readers can inspire minds to reflect and critique on a more open platform, and thus become seedbeds for rich and complex transactions. Our goal is that each student will initiate topics and questions within an undefined agenda, listen attentively and respond to others in mindful ways, maintain acceptable cultural conversation etiquette, and solve his own problems—even if that means seeking the help of a friend.

There are no roles assigned, no rigid, linear, controlled sequences of predictable events. This means that once the protocol is in place, students meet in a group that maintains ownership of its conversation, yet stays within the structure of the model. Because control rests in their hands (rather than the teacher's), they look to each other to make the decisions that will strengthen relationships within the collective. This undergirds the entire group and lays the structure for community.

The Content of a Literature Conversation

Yet, structure is not the only important facet. The content in the experience is just as valuable. First of all, literature conversations always maintain a text focus. That is, they evolve out of the content of a text, but the topic of focus can vary greatly between groups. These conversations, or dialogues, differ from discussions, in that discussions maintain a more formal structure (often one led by a teacher or a student-facilitator) and are usually about a particular topic (e.g., acid rain or westward expansion).

Furthermore, after three groups of students have listened to or read the same story, each group will often talk about different aspects and make far different connections to what was read. A conversation might flow from a particular text character to an unpredicted event to connections within the reader's own life. The trick is to stay on topic for a reasonable period of time before changing to another, which is again connected to what has been read or heard. It is this integrity to topic that helps develop the best conversations, for it evokes that deep, rich, reflective talk that always leaves me, the observer, in awe.

Sparked by issues related to morality, integrity, humanity, kindness, goodness, and evil, literature conversations are often fueled by a story's characters. Such conversations help lay the foundation needed for social, emotional, and moral development while circumventing a student's personal problems. That is, kids can identify and respond to a character without becoming that character or exposing personal or family issues. Indeed, the seeds of humor, empathy, and kindness are planted every day in a conversation community.

LITERATURE CONVERSATIONS: BETTER THAN FILLING IN SOMEONE ELSE'S BLANKS!

Boring workbooks, blackline masters, and other controlled devices—whose test-like nature calls for one right answer—could never evoke what conversations do. When students do the asking, the level of question depth is much greater, for kids tend to tackle the tough issues—ones whose answers must remain tentative. And they get caught up in it. That's why when literature is the core of conversations, students enjoy reading more. They follow authors, topics, and genres. They acquire tastes and preferences. They come to see reading not as assigned pages from a book with its accompanying workbook, but rather as a lifelong adventure.

AN INVITATION

I invite you to learn from my own developmental journey and that of my colleagues. Learn from our students through their transcribed voices. Join us! Create a conversation culture in your classroom. Enhance it with your own shades and hues.

In Step 1 you will learn how to help students observe, analyze, and investigate the workings of a real conversation—before they attempt one themselves. In Step 2, after a read-aloud in which the teacher models the process, students will experience "wondering" with a partner. Step 3 finds students in one large conversation circle, learning to refine content and behaviors for Step 4, which asks them to use the process without their teacher's presence within an interdependently functioning small group. In Step 5 students no longer rely on teacher read-alouds, but instead read independently for conversation grist, which will later help drive their group's interactions and assessments. Additionally, the Appendix provides rich textual resources to use during read-aloud modeling lessons as well as sample transcriptions that can serve as handy examples for instruction and assessment.

By following this step-by-step protocol, you can create a conversation community in your classroom. Invite your students into this culture of focused talk. Build relationships that grow healthy, happy, caring individuals, who will in turn help to create a healthier, happier, and more caring world.

KNEE TO KNEE, EYE TO EYE

Chapter 1

OBSERVING THE CONVERSATION PROCESS

Conversation is the cornerstone of civilization, the very essence of culture and community.
J. Walljasper, "The Power of Talk" (2002, 54)

When I first attempted literature conversations in my own classroom, I experienced one blunder after another. I tried everything! But nothing worked. The kids came out looking like little robots that always seemed to need their buttons pushed to continue operating. It took me two years to figure out what the problem was. That is, the kids did not even know what a real conversation looked like! After some pondering, I realized why that was.

NO TIME TO TALK

Today's society does not have time for conversations. People don't sit on their back porches and chat the evening away as they used to do. They don't even eat supper together much of the time. And we all know that school curricula have never been the seedbeds for growing open conversation among peers. You may say, "People have conversations all the time!" But I refer here to that deep, rich, reflective talk between and among people who maintain a common interest—*a time when individuals offer a spoken investment in a topic and in another human being.*

It is therefore little wonder that the implementation of these group book talks has baffled many teachers (and I speak from experience!). A lack of models would be a good reason to have difficulty in learning any process because, in order to become competent in any complex process, one must have an opportunity to watch someone else doing it. We hear people say over and over again: "Just show me." We learn to swim, read, and drive *after* we know what the task looks like. Thus, that's where we begin.

WHY KIDS NEED TO OBSERVE A REAL CONVERSATION

I've asked students to consider how conversations occur in their own lives, and regardless of the grade level, I have found that most of them have *very* minimal conversation experiences (either actual or vicarious). Although I have worked with children my entire life, I am continually taken aback by their responses to this inquiry. That is why it is of utmost importance to invite students to observe and analyze a conversation *before* they actually participate in one.

Yet, we must wonder, what has happened? Why are there no conversations? Students in most classrooms explain that they no longer have a period during a family meal to discuss or converse. This seemed hard to believe at first, so I investigated the topic with students at almost every grade level, and each time kids were hard put to come up with a period when they, or their families, have had extended conversation around a given topic. It just does not happen.

I ask, "Don't you talk while you're eating supper?" The answers generally fall into two categories: (1) kids eat at a separate time than their parents (and usually in front of the TV) or (2) the families eat together, but they do so in front of the TV, when no one is expected to interrupt programming.

"What about other times?" I ask. Again and again they insist that their family is too busy to have conversations. Adamant that there must be one time when this happens, I persist, "Don't you have conversations in the car while you are going from place to place?" Their responses usually reveal that the driver does not want to be interrupted or that they certainly are *not* going to talk to their siblings.

I ask kids about conversations with friends who come to visit. Most of them say that they and their friends do not talk; they play—or watch TV.

I know that school buses and lunchrooms do not support rich conversation. In lunchrooms conversation is impossible for one of two reasons: either (1) the kids are not allowed to talk or (2) everyone is shouting and the place is somewhat chaotic. Even in cafeterias that might lend an atmosphere for conversation, the possibilities are slim because of time limits; that is, most kids have half-hour lunch periods. If they get into an in-depth conversation, they will end up with a plateful of food that they did not have time to eat.

Therefore, asking students to recall conversation experiences—their own or others'—is usually fruitless. To participate in a conversation, students must possess the mental model, but where can they observe and analyze a real conversation?

FINDING A CONVERSATION MODEL

There are a number of ways one might obtain a conversation model for kids to observe and analyze. I have listed several here. Each has been used by the teachers with whom I have worked or by me. Some of them provide a more optimal experience, but all have worked at one time or another.

A videotaped conversation is by far the best tool because it allows for pausing the tape to discuss very small segments. I also like to rewind bits here and there for a re-viewing, which of course cannot be done with a live group. Also, I like to use the tape over and over. In this technological society with a Blockbuster on every corner, procuring a video with a segment of conversation should not be very difficult. But first, check the following list and see which avenue seems best.

WAYS TO OBTAIN A CONVERSATION MODEL

- The teacher can videotape parts of adult book club discussions. Barnes and Noble has regularly scheduled book talks. Inquire about taping one. A functioning adult book club should be easier to locate nowadays, because their numbers doubled, to around a half-million, from 1994 to 1998 (Jacobsohn 1998).
- Even better, many teachers are creating faculty book clubs at their schools. Why not tape a portion of one?

Observing the Conversation Process

- Conversations and discussions can be taped from television or the Internet and then shown to the students for analyzing. As a matter of fact, the *Oprah* show, perhaps the greatest historical incentive to book talks, has monthly adult book clubs. However, consider the content carefully first. Furthermore, Oprah.com offers book talk video segments from those monthly dialogues, many of which include the book's author.
- Some students do have miniconversations during their lunch period each day at school. If they do, why not send them off with pencil, paper, and guidelines, encouraging them to analyze and observe what makes their lunchtime conversations successful? This one worked well for some City of Buffalo teachers last year.
- Another possibility is to rent a video that you have scanned for a conversation. It is not necessary that it be a lengthy interaction. *Even a few minutes is fine.* Some of the older family movies have more conversations than newer, faster moving films. One that I like for this purpose is from the *Ramona* series (Cleary), and it contains two stories, the first of which I have found works pretty well. It is called "Mystery Meal" and contains a segment close to the beginning of the tape that finds the family in the kitchen involved in a normal-looking conversation. It is important that the conversation look normal and *not staged.* Another video with a fairly rich conversation right at the beginning is *Joe Gould's Secret* by October Films (2000).
- While I was presenting a series of conversation workshops to Buffalo teachers, one creative teacher, who had special teachers scheduled in her classroom each day, collaborated with them in setting up a literature conversation demonstration. After a shared, whole-class listening experience, three teachers gathered into a triad in front of the students to show them the workings of a conversation. They even invited an interested student in, making the group a quad!
- I always recommend that teachers videotape conversations from each year's class to use as an example for later classes. For this reason, I have a treasury of them.

The photo at this chapter's beginning shows students at Buffalo's International School investigating a videotaped conversation while a scribe takes notes and I guide the interactions. I hope teachers working toward a conversation curriculum will be able to copy, rent, or purchase such a videotape of a conversation. Without a model it may take all year to get the students on the right track. Yet once they observe and analyze a real conversation, the next step slides in place quite nicely.

EXPLAINING THE PROCESS

Students need to know why they'll be viewing a conversation before they enter the event. Therefore, the first thing I do is explain how tough it is when we try a process in which we have little or no experience. I select a sport about which I know little and explain the strange way I might play it, having never experienced it before. For instance, if I have never seen someone play hockey, I might use the stick as a baseball bat. Of course everyone is laughing by the time I'm finished, but the students get the idea.

ACTIVE LISTENING AND FOCUSED RESPONSE

Meg Wheatley suggests that "the greatest barrier to good conversation is that we've lost the capacity to listen. We're too busy, too certain, too stressed . . . We just keep rushing past each other . . ." (2002, 31). Consequently, we need to demonstrate new ways of being for our students. We begin with two important elements.

Active listening and *focused response* are the keys to the synergistic interactions that take place in conversations. Synergistic conversations resemble complex talk-dances. That is, participants are completely consumed within the topic *and* each other. *Salons* (Sandra and Spayde 2001) explains that "Shelley Kessler, who has taught council method to elementary school students, advocated listening 'between the lines' as someone speaks, 'hearing the feelings and intentions as well as the words' " (101). Thus, participants finish each other's sentences, mirror the gestures of other group members, back off and reenter with grace and finesse, and examine a topic from a variety of avenues, grounding their thoughts in sound evidence. This kind of intensity does not usually occur throughout an entire conversation, but ebbs and flows, riding on the group's waves of interest. In the end, participants frequently come away from such an experience inspired and richer than they were beforehand. Such active listening and focused response is exactly what we want a class to observe before diving into a literature conversation themselves.

Once the context for such a synergistic interaction is constructed or acquired, I encourage the class to investigate and assess that conversation for what's making it work. And, in the case of video viewing, I describe how we will be seeing only small segments at a time so we can stop to discuss the tiny details of each piece of footage. When observers notice something that is making the process work, we write it on a Conversation Tips chart in order to remember it and use it ourselves. This is a most important and ongoing facet of the process; that is, this chart is referenced and developed throughout the year.

I don't spend too much time on this pre-viewing explanation because the kids always better understand once they get into the observation process.

DEVELOPING A CONVERSATION TIPS CHART

Providing Goals for Viewing

Before we begin analyzing a conversation, it's helpful, if the circumstances allow, for the class to see it in its entirety, that is, without any interruptions. Even more important is to provide some viewing or observation guidelines, so that they will notice something besides an interesting shirt that someone is wearing. A few pre-viewing questions will direct their focus; however, it's best to keep the number down to three or four. Following are some that work well for me.

PRE-VIEWING QUESTIONS

- What is happening that makes these conversations work?
- What are the peoples' bodies doing as they talk (their gestures)?
- What kinds of things are they saying? What are they talking about?
- How are the people acting toward each other? How are they treating each other?

Inside a Literature Conversation: What Will We See?

At first, students have a difficult time noticing behaviors, even after the pre-viewing question prompts. But, so have teachers during workshops I've presented! We all have to learn how to look, teachers and students alike. Furthermore, because analyzing is more difficult in the first stages, it's best to begin with a brief section—maybe thirty to forty seconds long—before stopping for students to share their observations. That's why videos work best, because each time I hit pause on the VCR, I can offer one of the aforementioned pre-viewing questions. Yet these frequent pauses would have to wait until the end if students were observing an actual, live conversation, where such interruptions would become intrusions.

When using a videotaped conversation, I also find it helps to rewind brief sections of the footage—sometimes several times—while continually asking, "What do you notice this time that's making the conversation work?" (Although there are negative aspects of every conversation, we do not draw attention to those.) After about ten minutes, students catch on to what is expected, and their comments generally become more astute. That is, viewers become more observant, noting the finer details within the interactions and the content. It's really quite amazing how students can re-view a conversation and each time experience a different response.

What are these things they notice? What should a teacher and her class expect to observe while viewing a conversation?

Observing Gestures: A Top Priority

It becomes quickly evident that gestural behaviors predominate. When all is said and done, the gestural content of conversations makes up the majority of our observations. Watching a video on mute can be very revealing—and may even be a good place to start with the kids. It's pretty amazing how much we can learn from just a person's body language.

Gestures may be silent, and almost instinctual, but they play a leading part in the message being conveyed. Linguists (people who study language) suggest that we receive around 90 percent of our meaning through gestures (PBS 1995). Accordingly, 55 percent of the speaker's message is contained in visual, not verbal, cues. Another 38 percent goes to the vocal qualities of tone, pitch, and pace. Griffin (2001) attributes only 7 percent of the message to the words!

This is probably why kids notice qualities like eye contact and hand movements first. And well they should, for the unspoken message is all too clear: if you aren't looking at me, you're probably not listening. They also notice more general gestural references, and so they comment, "He's paying attention," and "She's a good listener," to which I respond, "What do you mean? What is happening that makes you say that?" In this way, we get right down to the nitty-gritty. What exactly are the conversation participants doing? What exactly do active listeners do that qualifies them as active listeners?

This gestural focus is important, because such cues often become the message that can help us win a spouse, a job, or even a presidency! Reason enough to study gesture. Yet how many of us would actually consider it as an important aspect of the language arts? Perhaps it's time to reconsider.

Gesture Differences Between Groups

When observing conversations in action, some have noticed specific patterns related to certain groups. Deborah Tannen (1990) states that during conversation, the behaviors of males and females differ so much that "in many ways, second-grade girls were more like twenty-five-year-old women than like the second-grade boys" (245). She says that, in general, boys

- are more restless;
- are continually aware of the hierarchical framework they're in;
- will mock and resist their semiconfinement;
- show affection through an oppositional format (i.e., bumping, poking); and
- more directly disagree.

On the other hand, girls

- comply with an authoritarian framework;
- interact by agreeing with and supporting each other; and
- reassure group members that they are successfully complying.

Many who read Tannen's conclusions would respond, "So what's new? Boys are still being boys." But, in regard to literature conversations, I feel compelled to revise Tannen's findings, because such book-centered dialogues possess some important ingredients that her groups did not have, and accordingly, they sport far different results—the kind of results that indicate focus and engagement. The kind of results that may create a more caring, understanding citizen. And the kind of results that nurture deep, reflective reading of text.

Freedom Within Parameters

For the most part, those specific gender differences are not as obvious when teachers use the *Knee to Knee, Eye to Eye* protocol. That is, boys *do* make eye contact and invite others in. They *do* stay put and stay focused—even in second grade. Why do these results differ from Tannen's? The answer bears important clues to successful literature conversations.

First of all, Tannen's were observations of free conversations with no student preparation; that is, kids received no *specific guidelines* and were therefore not certain of what they were supposed to be doing. Whereas the protocol we use does indeed have such guidelines (but not roles), and students are scaffolded through that structure step-by-step in a way that lays a path to self-control—or better yet, *engaged responsibility*.

The second issue is related to the *content* of the task. Literature conversations have content freedom within parameters. That is, students have the freedom to change the subject, but it must still be related to the book in some way, whereas Tannen's students were offered a very nebulous topic ("Talk about something serious.") whose parameters were almost limitless. In book talks the topic is the text. Anchored there, conversation should not go far astray, as it did for Tannen's kids.

I believe another important factor is that during a literature conversation, all members have essentially had the same experience, and students are therefore *bound by a common parcel of knowledge*. This provides a fundamental level of security, a grounding. Plus, it makes it easier to support and extend another's ideas, for most group members have "been there and done that."

These elements are important observations that can be brought out during the viewing. As a consequence, I have heard observers offer comments such as "They are staying on the topic," and "They all seem like they know what they're doing," and "They are all talking about the book," or "They look like they care about each other."

These are indeed important observations, not only for literature conversations but also for life in general. It therefore seems reasonable to hypothesize that if students have several years of literature conversation experiences, they will be better prepared to one day work amicably with other employees, keep their marriage on steady ground, and even negotiate peace treaties with foreign diplomats. Who's to say where talent in conversation might lead?

Observing Feedback

Actually, one of the most important aspects of literature conversations that we want students to notice is the sensitive and related feedback others give to peers' comments and questions. I even use that term, *feedback*, with upper elementary students. If they have studied feedback loops in science or other curricular areas, they can stretch those connections into conversation behaviors. However, other terms, such as *respond, answer, give back*, or *piggyback*, also work well. Outside of active listening (which can also be feedback), such student-to-student engaged response is the key to good conversation.

Taking turns—not!

A related and interesting observation that arises early in almost every classroom (and even in some teacher workshops) involves the statement "They are taking turns." Not really! People do not *actually* take turns in a conversation—maybe in a discussion, but not in a dialogue. This is quite obvious when we observe one. As soon as I ask the students, "Are they *really* taking turns? Is one person talking and then the next in line and then the next?" they realize that, although classroom discipline charts suggest such behavior, conversation does not involve taking turns. Most groups ponder this carefully, and some of their most valuable and interesting comments arise from this one conundrum: if they're not taking turns, then what are they doing?

Overlapping

Overlap occurs when two or more individuals are speaking at the same time. Tannen (1990) suggests that the most important consideration in overlap is whether "a speaker is violating another speaker's rights"; however, in order to make such a judgment, listeners "have to know a lot about both the speakers and the situation" (190). We need to ask students to consider two things: (1) the effect that the interruption might have on the speaker as well as (2) the content of the second speaker's comment. Was it related? Was it supportive? We talk about the following questions, and then I scribe the students' observations onto our growing Conversation Tips chart.

QUESTIONS TO VALIDATE ACCEPTABLE OVERLAPPING

- Did the overlap reinforce the speaker's content?
- Did the overlap extend the speaker's content?
- Did the overlap contradict the speaker's content?
- Did the overlap change the topic on the floor?

Interrupting or piggybacking?

I have a special term for responses that extend the speaker's content. I call it *piggybacking.* Kids love that term, and it comes in handy throughout the school day.

Sometimes I, or a student, step back and ask someone, "Are you interrupting or are you piggybacking?" Even kindergartners know the difference and, therefore, respond accordingly.

Basically, kids just need to know that their primary task during literature conversations is to provide sensitive and related feedback or response. I think knowing that their primary responsibility centers on feedback, rather than on wondering, paves the road for mindful interaction.

To clarify this further, let's consider some real responses, transcribed from a videotape. The following overlaps were made by Kirsten Baetzhold's third graders after listening to a chapter from *Roll of Thunder, Hear My Cry*. Does what occurs seem to be an interruption or is someone piggybacking? Remember: piggybacking extends or clarifies the previous person's comment. Interruptions do not, because their owners have an agenda of their own.

I find it very helpful, in general—not only during literature conversations—to have kids wrestle with the differences between interruptions and piggybacking. Try using the following examples to do just that.

Example 1:

> *Responder 1:* 'Cause he said his leg got blown off—
>
> *Responder 2:* *Almost* blown off.

Example 2:

> *Responder 1:* Yeah, like Stacy said, "You just don't understand."
>
> *Responder 2:* It's like—
>
> *Responder 3:* She could have got burnt.

Example 3:

> *Responder 1:* Yeah! That's why he was limping.
>
> *Responder 2:* It said in the book he was limping. It was his left leg—
>
> *Responder 3:* [*reading*] "Standing firmly on his left leg."
>
> *Responder 4:* Yeah!

Even first graders learn to handle interruptions, as can be seen in the following example from Leigh-Ann Hildreth's room. This group had just used *The Great*

Kapok Tree as a shared reading text and was discussing it, making repeated use of the illustrations. Notice what happens when participants pull them off topic:

Willow:	Why can't he sleep over here [*pointing*]?
Tenisha:	Because there's a leopard on the branch.
Tula:	Yeah, and some leopards eat people.
Vinnie:	Yeah, leopards eat people. And some leopard seals eat people.
Tenisha:	No they don't!
Vinnie:	Yeah, they do.
Tenisha:	No! Seals don't eat people!
Tula:	We're getting off the topic.

It's both fun and helpful to invite students to investigate the inside of this process by using transcriptions like the ones here. That is, show them examples of transcriptions (see the Appendix) and call for individuals to read particular parts, much like a radio play. After reading through once in a natural manner, we go back and reread each interaction separately to evaluate the response's type and validity, as we continually consider: is the person piggybacking or interrupting? Such investigations have positive repercussions.

SCRIBING POSITIVE OBSERVATIONS ON A CONVERSATIONS TIPS CHART

Who's Scribing?

In classrooms of fluent writers, I select a competent student to scribe our observations onto a class chart, so that I can concentrate on leading the discussion. I always suggest to any scribe, "Don't worry too much about how the chart looks, because we will copy it over into a more final product later." Student scribes are especially helpful when I'm using a video, because it frees my hands to press pause at the appropriate time and place.

However, student scribing may not be feasible in classrooms of emergent writers, and thus the teacher must assume a more multiple role. At the end of the session, even if I was the scribe, I ask for a volunteer to be responsible for copying over our edited and revised work-in-progress into a more legible format.

A student at City of Buffalo's International School scribes our dictations as we analyze a conversation video.

Constructing a Positive How-To Chart

Whether the teacher or a student logs the observations made by the class, it is essential these remain positive and "how-to" or rule-like in nature. In other words, grammatically they should appear to be a set of *positive* commands. For instance:

◆ Avoid interrupting.
◆ Look at the person speaking.
◆ Be patient.

Setting this positive focus right from the beginning will, in the long run, simplify the task. When a student does offer a negative statement, such as "Don't interrupt," I might stop and invite that student and the class to revise by turning the statement into its positive form. For example, "Don't interrupt!" may transform into "Wait to talk until someone finishes." However, sometimes doing revision in the middle of the observation process holds us back. So instead, I often simply log whatever the students say, and then we go back later and revise.

I have a little trick that I use that seems to help the kids stay focused. As a constant reminder to stay away from negatives, such as using the word *not* as well as words that have *n't* in them, I use a "no smoking" symbol. This is also helpful when we are constructing rubrics.

Why All the Fuss About Keeping It Positive?

The reason it's so imperative to keep statements positive is because student observations will be scribed onto chart paper and kept as guidelines and eventual sources for assessment descriptors. Furthermore, it is always better to know what *to do*, rather than what *not to do*. There will always be thousands of things that one should not do, but once we state what to do, it narrows the field of negatives. That is, we might write on our chart: "Listen to the person talking." This automatically obviates many negative behaviors, so that we don't have to state, "Don't talk when someone else is talking," "Don't interrupt," or "Do not leave the group." For if we are truly listening to the person talking, it is obvious we are not involved in any of those other behaviors. I explain this to the kids.

Even so, staying positive is often the toughest part for students who are trying to interpret what they have observed, and many teachers have shared with me their own difficulties and frustrations in trying to get the kids to circumvent the negatives. This, unfortunately, points to a school culture that is acclimated toward "Thou shall nots."

The good news is that, in working with children in grades K–5, I have noticed that the more we attempt to restate and revise those negativities, the more we get down into the real nitty-gritty of what makes a conversation work. The outcome is definitely worth our struggles, for it gradually connects our hours together with a new kind of self-discipline and its accompanying interaction vocabulary. Whatever happens in your own room, trust the kids.

The Neverending Conversations Tips Chart

Furthermore, the chart is never really finished anyway, because we continue to add to it all year long. Every time we discover something new that makes conversations work well, we add it to the initial list. Within a four-month period, Sheila Delmonte's second grade at Heritage Heights in Sweet Home collected three large chart pages of positive observations!

A Maplemere teacher, Amy Patterson, and I were also really pleased with her second graders' midyear observation chart. Amy and her class formed a community

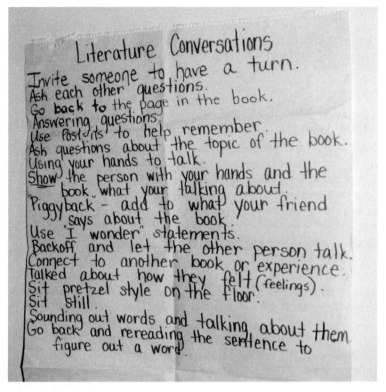

A Conversation Tips chart created by Amy Patterson's second graders

spirit early on, so it was easier for them to analyze what they saw working in the conversation they viewed. Note the photo of the list from Amy's class above.

I have been discussing a number of considerations related to observing conversations to construct a guidance chart, but often the understanding of a process such as this is made easier when presented in a different manner—one that more closely aligns with showing, rather than telling. Perhaps the following (fictitious) vignettes will better depict what the process would look and sound like in a classroom. These vignettes will bring Step 1 to life. Although the first vignette takes place in a kindergarten and the second in a fourth grade, they might well occur in any classroom.

CLASSROOMS IN ACTION:
OBSERVING A LIVE CONVERSATION COMMUNITY

Mrs. Gentner wanted to have her kindergartners begin talking more about books. She wanted to show them what a book conversation looks like, but decided that by the time she orchestrated the model or located a video, months would pass. She pondered, Where are there conversations going on that we could observe? Allowing this question to sit in the back of her mind for awhile eventually evoked an answer: the cafeteria! That was it! It might not offer the best examples, but it was still a place to begin.

The idea steeped for the rest of that day, and by evening she had begun making her plan. The next morning she stopped by the cafeteria to check in with Mr. Uga, asking if it would be a problem if, during the fifth-grade lunch, her class came into the cafeteria and stood on the far end to observe.

Mr. Uga, who always seemed to adore the kindergartners, responded, "Sure! The more the merrier!"

Next, Mrs. Gentner stopped by the fifth grades to ask those teachers to let their kids know that the kindergartners would be coming in to observe "the big kids" during lunch. She also asked the teachers, "Could you remind the kids to just be themselves and do what they always do? We simply want to watch how fifth graders talk to each other."

When the kindergartners came to the morning meeting on the rug that day, Mrs. Gentner excitedly shared her idea. "I want us to begin talking about books, so I've been trying to think of a way that we could all watch what people look like when they are having a conversation—when they are talking to each other. I thought we might try observing the big kids in the cafeteria while they have lunch, and look what I made for us!" She pulled a stack of large cardboard pieces shaped like magnifying glasses out of her bag. The children's attention immediately became focused, as they more closely examined the large shapes.

"I'm going to give each of you a pretend magnifying glass so that you can be a conversation detective. How many of you have ever watched a baby or a dog or an ant very closely?" Most of the children raised their hands and some began to share related experiences. Mrs. Gentner picked up a magnifying glass and looked through it to gain their attention again before she continued, "Yes, well, when you observe anything very closely we could say you are being a detective, because detectives observe things closely and then remember what they saw and heard. Do you think you could do that?"

Excitedly, the class responded, "Ye-e-e-e-s!"

"But before we use these, I want each of you to reach into the hat I have here and select the detective team you will be on. Everyone will get to be on a team, but each team will be watching something different," the teacher explained as she walked over to a chart she had prepared earlier.

"Here are the observation teams," she said, pointing to a list of words with pictures of body parts beside each. "There will be a team for each of these. Maybe you can even help me read this list of teams," Mrs. Gentner invited, knowing that the pictures would give the clues to decoding the words. As she slid her hand under each word, she read, "Eye detectives. Head detectives. Hand detectives. Body detectives. Talk detectives."

Turning to the group again, she went on, "Now, each of you will be on one of these teams. If you are on the eye detective team, what do you suppose you will be very closely watching?"

"Them's eyes!" shouted Michael, always eager to please.

"Right," responded Mrs. Gentner. "Their eyes. But I want to explain just a bit more. When we come back to the room, we will be talking about what was happening while the kids were talking. Where were they looking with their eyes when they were talking? What were their heads doing? Their hands? Their bodies? And if you are on the talk team, you will be carefully observing who talked the most and who may not have talked at all. Watch carefully."

"I am going to let each of you come up to get your magnifying glass and pick a team out of the hat, and when you go to your table, please use your crayons to make a picture for your team on the handle of your pretend magnifying glass. So, if you are on the eyes team, what will you draw?"

"Eyes!" the group quickly responded, eager to get started.

The children came forward, one at a time, to reach into the hat and draw out a captioned picture, while Mrs. Gentner asked again and again, "What team are you on?" Each child responded accordingly.

When the class was ready, Mrs. Gentner gave the final directions, "Okay, when we get down there, we will all be as quiet as possible so we can be top-notch detectives, and also so we don't bother the fifth graders. Detectives are always very quiet people. Just stand against the wall and use your magnifying glass to focus on your team's special thing."

However, before they left the room, their teacher did a quick simulation, by having the kids focus on a brief interaction between her and a parent volunteer. When the children seemed to adequately understand the procedure, they all moved quietly down the hallway.

As the kindergartners began lining the cafeteria wall, the fifth graders stopped to watch, and when the younger children lifted their magnifying glasses, a few snickers could be heard here and there. But soon the older children forgot all about the young observers and went about their normal lunchtime chattering.

When the kindergarten children returned to their own room, Mrs. Gentner asked them to put the magnifying glasses at their tables and come to the rug. She then began discussing what people do when they are talking to someone. She took their responses in no special order, but scaffolded some children who had difficulty explaining what they saw. As the children dictated, their teacher took notes on a large chart, and after they dictated several observations, the teacher invited, "Help me read what you said people do during a conversation." Accordingly, Mrs. Gentner tracked the print as she and the group read the following:

- They watched each other.
- Their heads looked at the talking person.
- They moved their hands a lot.
- They sat still while they were talking.
- They smiled a lot.
- First one talked and then someone talked to them.

Mrs. Gentner was satisfied with their novice beginning, knowing full well that they would be building on their list all year long. She knew that some of the most important elements for a kindergarten conversation were already on that list, and she therefore felt comfortable to move on to the next step the following day.

CLASSROOMS IN ACTION: CREATING A CONVERSATION TIPS CHART

It was September in Mrs. Donati's fourth grade. Everyone was still getting to know one another, but their teacher could see that some cliques were already starting to form. She decided there was no time like the present to implement literature conversations. So, she called the class to their meeting area and explained her plan:

"We have some pretty interesting books in our room, and we'll be participating in book clubs before long. You know, when I read a good book, I always search for a friend who has also read it, so that I can talk with her about it. That's what you too will be doing this year—talking with friends about what you're reading," informed Mrs. Donati. "Conversations are something that we can experience in a variety of places. How many of you have conversations at the supper table at home?"

Only a few children raised their hands. Mrs. Donati called on some of them to share the kinds of things they talked about during supper. She then asked the class another question (primarily for those who did not raise their hands): "How many of you had a conversation with a friend today at lunch?" Most of the children indicated an affirmative response. She then called on some of them to share their lunchtime topics.

"So, you can see that we all have experiences in conversing with others. But I want us to get really good at having deep, rich, and interesting conversations. So the first thing we are going to do is watch a video of some readers who are involved in a conversation about a book they have all read. As you view the video, be thinking about the four questions I have written on the board. Let's talk a bit about what they mean," suggested Mrs. Donati. She then ran her hand under the first question (see page 6 for pre-viewing questions) and offered some ideas to the group. Next she invited, "Would anyone else like to add something to extend my thoughts on this topic?" Two children offered personal experiences, and then Mrs. Donati moved on to each of the other questions in the same manner.

When the class finished discussing the questions, their teacher suggested, "We will need to share the good things we view on the tape, so when I press pause, be ready with some positive observations." She went on to advise that they keep track of their observations by scribing them onto a chart, and then she asked, "Would you please point to someone in our room who could be a good scribe for us—someone who spells easily and whose handwriting we will be able to read?" Students pointed primarily to three of their classmates. A significant number pointed to Meagan, so Mrs. Donati asked, "Meagan, it looks like your classmates think you can do a good job of being our scribe, and I agree. What do you say? Would you feel comfortable writing for us?" Meagan smiled as she shyly accepted the compliment. Then she stood, prepared to begin.

Mrs. Donati had chart paper ready on the opposite side of the room, and she handed Meagan some colored markers. As a final thought, she added, "Now, Meagan, if you come across a tough word, don't be afraid to ask us for help. We're here if you need us."

As Meagan walked toward the chart, Mrs. Donati moved to the television monitor and the VCR, turned both on, and pushed the videotape into its slot. Viewing began. On the tape one student had just made a comment and another had answered him, so Mrs. Donati pressed pause and asked, "What is making this conversation work so far?"

Michael's hand shot up first. "Michael?" responded the teacher.

"Well, that one kid answered the other one," Michael offered.

"Yes, now how should we state that on our chart, so that it will remind us what to do?" asked Mrs. Donati.

Michael thought for a second and responded, "Answer kids when they talk to you."

"A great beginning!" celebrated Mrs. Donati, "Oh—and I see that Meagan has already begun writing Michael's words on the chart. Thanks, Meagan, you're doing a great job!"

"What else did you notice?" the teacher inquired again, this time going back to the pre-viewing questions and pointing to each as she read, "What are the kids' bodies doing as they talk? What kind of things . . . ?"

After another child dictated that "the kids on the tape are sitting together," Meagan wrote it on the chart, and Mrs. Donati hit play to continue viewing. After about a half-minute, she again stopped the tape and led a similar pattern of discussion and scribed statements.

Fifteen minutes into the activity, Mrs. Donati noticed that more children were now wanting to share observations. Plus, the observations were becoming more refined and focused, which meant they would make great guidelines for future conversations. So, the teacher shared this with the group: "Wow! You observers are really going at it now! And I bet you can find many different descriptors to add to our chart!" This comment appeared to add zest to an already committed audience.

After about a half-hour, Mrs. Donati said, "Let's stop here for today. We've really collected lots of great ideas that will help us with our own conversations. Let's try to remember these each time we discuss books—or anything else—with each other. In the upcoming days we'll be watching more of the video and adding to our chart. But we, ourselves, will be getting experience in talking about books, too. As a matter of fact, tomorrow I have a great book to read to you, and we'll try some partner conversations then. Just remember all those good things we observed and talked about today."

A student in Heidi Clarke's fourth grade hangs their Conversation Tips chart for handy reference.

NOW THAT WE'VE EXPERIENCED A CONVERSATION

After experiencing this first step, students are always eager to begin the process themselves. Both they and the teacher usually want to dive right in. However, we're not ready for diving yet. But, in Chapter 2, we do wade in up to our ankles in an atmosphere of modeling, support, and practice.

Chapter 2

DYNAMIC DUOS
WONDERING WITH A PARTNER

Ignorance is not so much not knowing an answer as not knowing that there is a question, not being able to think when thinking is required.
Frank Smith, Essays into Literacy (1983, 1)

I love this step, probably because it is here that the pieces start falling together. That is, kids actually begin conversing with a partner about a piece of literature. It's fun to watch them get caught up in each other and the topic. Most slide into the process with ease because they now have the mental framework that supports what they're doing; that is, they've observed and analyzed a real conversation *before* being asked to do it themselves. Plus, they have their guidelines chart.

So, they can begin to model what they've seen. Yet it's still best to move slowly, using a strong social structure, rich read-alouds, and lots of teacher modeling. With that in mind, we move into Step 2, which begins with *wondering*.

Researchers say that questioning is at the core of comprehension (Harvey and Goudvis 2000; Burns, Griffin, and Snow 1999; Beck et al. 1997; Cunningham and Allington 1994; Weaver 1988; Anderson et al. 1985). Furthermore, most who are seriously involved in adult book clubs say that questioning is central to a good book discussion. Mortimer Adler, Great Books advocate, suggests three basic questions readers should ask: What's the author saying? What does the author mean? How close to the truth is it? (Jacobsohn 1998). Elliot Bay, an enormous Seattle bookstore, has a website offering a very lengthy list of questions that can become the grist for book-related conversations. And almost every top-selling novel now has a list of discussion questions after the story.

All of this connects to the way in which good literature is used in today's society. We may decide to eventually offer some of these prompts to our kids, but for now, let's not succumb to structured prompts. Besides, questioning does not involve only the text.

Meg Wheatley (2002) suggests that curiosity is the foundation of a good conversation—but for another reason. She carries questioning one step further.

> Curiosity helps us discard our mask and let down our guard. It creates a spaciousness that is rare in other interactions. It takes time to create this space, but as we feel it growing, we speak more truthfully and the conversation moves into what's real. (30)

Wheatley means we need to be curious, not only about the topic and its content but also about the thoughts of others who are in conversation with us. She explains that "curiosity and good listening bring us back together" into community (36). Indeed, curiosity, questioning, and wonderment not only give rise to conversations but also keep them going.

Where do we begin? Let's simply use our own good minds and model the wonders that just naturally bubble up. Even a very young child wonders.

EVEN PRESCHOOLERS QUESTION TEXT!

Children are born with curiosity coursing through their veins. From a very early age they investigate their environment and question it. Preschoolers fortunate enough to have book experiences with an adult just naturally continue their intellectual inquisitions within the context of text. Even at twenty-two months, Cameron questions many pages of one of his favorite books. "*Fweight Twain* by Donowd Kwooz" (*Freight Train* by Donald Crews), Cameron mimics. However, aware of the limits of his own color knowledge, Cameron's voice lilts upward as he questioningly glances at his mom each time he "reads" a page with a color on it.

"Wed tank caw?" Cameron's voice and glance ask, as he points to the sentence from right to left.

"*Orange* tank car," his mom reads, offering the correct model and stressing the color word.

At three, Delanie sits for her bedtime stories with Grandma, who is reading *The Napping House* by Audrey and Don Wood, a patterned book whose cover and cumulative structure evidence a growing pile of characters sleeping on top of Granny. On the second page Delanie points to the picture of a sleeping child on a chair and asks, "Why is him sleeping on that chair?" No doubt she is wondering why has the boy collapsed in the *chair*, if the characters are going to pile on top of the *bed*. Inference, a key comprehension skill, generates a question at the age of three!

It's easy to see that book conversations can occur at a very early age. Therefore, for some, school literature conversations will be a continuation of a process already begun; for others, we will have to do more modeling.

INVITING WONDERS

The easiest way to get a conversation going is to create an environment that honors wondering. I start out by talking to the students about the wonders that I myself have had. Real ones! I offer them everything I wondered while driving to school that day. I say, "Do you ever wonder about things that are happening? Sometimes I practically drown myself with wonders. Today when I was driving to school I wondered whether there are as many deer living in the wooded area near my home as there were a few years ago; why my car smells a little different today; what model car was in front of me; and when the county is going to start the anticipated road renovation. Sometimes I figure out the answers to my wonders right away. But there are lots of times when I never find the answer. Does that ever happen to you?"

I then invite the class to share some of their own morning wonders, which usually evokes some light humor. Throughout, we are creating an environment that validates wondering as a natural experience, one that I sometimes call *constructive daydreaming*.

I do not contain my wonders within only the reading realm, though. I demonstrate for the group at a variety of times that it is appropriate to wonder during any experience—a field trip, a videotape, an experiment, a play, and so on. That's what deep thinking is all about! So we continually make room for wondering across our day together.

USING REAL WONDERS FOR GUIDED COMPREHENSION

Once kids have related wondering to experiences outside of school, we can move on to wonders associated with school texts, which we call *text response*. As I prepare lessons that will model text-related wondering for the class, I consider carefully the kinds of inquiries I am offering, because these beginning wonders set the stage for the entire process.

Most important, I never demonstrate text-response wonders that might be found on traditional comprehension exercises—wonders like "What color is her cape?" or "Where is Little Red Riding Hood going?" or "Why is Little Red Riding Hood taking bread in a basket?" Sandra and Spayde (2001) suggest that questions should *stimulate, not direct*. Real (or honest) wonders do stimulate; thus, they drive and guide the process.

On the other hand, pretend (directive) queries about a text have come to be known as *teacher questions*, because the teacher actually knows the answers before he asks the question. Such questions are testlike and even intimidating. They do not stimulate. They lead kids to draw a line of demarcation separating the real world with its real questions from school with its teacher questions (for more on this, see Shirley Brice Heath's 1983 *Ways with Words*). We want students to reflect deeply and sincerely both in and out of school. We don't want them to think that what we do in school is a kind of game that has to be learned and is played only under the roof of such institutions. Therefore, the kinds of questions I model must be heartfelt, pondered, rich, and real. This is so important.

Rather than offer, as an example, some of my own real wonders, let me share a few honest wonders from students in Heidi Clarke's fourth grade. After independently reading a chapter from *Toliver's Travels*, a book about colonialism and the Revolution, students had the following honest wonders. (Please note that, for the sake of brevity, each of these was pulled from its dialogical context.)

> *Sim:* On this page they say the redcoats—they live in this house and they're all patriots and I'm wondering, are the redcoats listening because they heard rustling upstairs. It says in paragraph 3: "They stood still and listened. She heard no stirring of the redcoats upstairs." But, I was wondering that—if there really was a redcoat up there?

Asa: On page 6 and 7: "He was yelling at her in a *gruff* voice?" What was he so mad about?

Nala: I wonder what the message said. Like, maybe the message is about something that's gonna happen.

ASKING QUESTIONS: A KEY COMPREHENSION STRATEGY

It is evident why wondering or questioning is a foundational comprehension strategy. The questions of Sim, Asa, and Nala demonstrate what occurs when students get used to ferreting out the meanings in text. They learn to use strategic questions—ones that demonstrate possible inferences, connections, syntheses, and predictions.

As a matter of fact, those who have studied how to get meaning from text (Stauffer 1969; Beck et al. 1997; Keene and Zimmerman 1997; Harvey and Goudvis 2000) contend questioning the text or the author is a basic comprehension strategy. Sandra and Spayde (2001), authors who have researched adult book talks, tell us that "questions are your way into the book" (155). This is just as true for kids.

The following steps provide a protocol that is grounded in guided comprehension with a special emphasis on questioning. However, other comprehension strategies will also eventually be woven into the guided comprehension protocol.

GUIDED COMPREHENSION

Literature conversation depends on understanding the text. Without comprehension, book-related discussions are next to impossible; that is, comprehension inspires conversation. Working in tandem with this idea, I approach the teaching of literature conversations through a guided comprehension methodology. The term *guided* inherently connotes support with demonstration. Therefore, throughout the journey into conversations, we teachers model strategies first, then invite the kids into the process, and eventually wean them off our support.

Through this guided comprehension model, students learn how to question text, make connections to their reading, infer and predict, analyze, critique, and synthesize. And the best part is, we use no boring workbooks or blackline masters!

The guided comprehension emphasis in this chapter is questioning or wondering, but, unlike traditional reading protocols, this one invites the kids to ask the questions. Very often it is this wondering about text that prompts other comprehension strategies to take root. That is, the questioning of text causes us to predict, to infer, or to analyze more closely. That's why this step is so important.

THE TEXT USED FOR MODELING

It is best—even for older students—to begin with a common piece of high-quality literature that is read aloud. Carefully selecting those first read-aloud texts is of utmost importance. They should be bursting with the kind of mystery, intrigue, and quandaries that beg listeners to wonder and predict. There is none better than the works of Chris Van Allsburg. His books *Just a Dream* and *The Wreck of the Zephyr* are two excellent examples that steep students in wonderment, even when they've previously heard or read them! Furthermore, Van Allsburg's work lends itself to any age—even adults. Also check the Appendix of this book for a listing of other good real-alouds.

Although, from the first page, Van Allsburg's books elicit evocative wonders, for many other books we must wait until we are further into them before the wonders start to bubble forth. Frequently, the story's beginning simply paints the setting, while the end answers all the questions. In other words, with most books there will be definite sections that evoke the richest wonders; therefore, an at-home trial run by the teacher will help pave the path to a more successful beginning. I adhere sticky notes to each part in the book to remind me later during the demonstration lesson where I found a good wonder. That way, as I am reading aloud I can just follow my preplanned cues.

Once I have formally modeled my own text wonders for the kids, they are ready to wonder or question. Thus, the process is set in place with specific expectations.

THE SOCIAL STRUCTURE: DYNAMIC DUOS

The least complicated conversation structure involves only two individuals. This means, at all times, one of them will be listening while the other will be talking—ideally, a fifty-fifty proposition. It's far easier to enter a conversation when your only competition is one person. The more individuals participating, the more complicated interactions become. That is why we begin with dyadic structures (partner sharing) in a whole-group setting, which enables the teacher to model and direct these initial lessons (see B in Figure 2–1).

Students in Leigh-Ann Hildreth's first grade go knee to knee in response to the teacher's read-aloud.

During most read-aloud experiences in my own room, I invite partners to join me in an area that will allow them to sit both face to face and alongside their classmate. In crowded classrooms that have no common area, students can partner at their desks. I like to begin by asking the kids to select their own partners. Self-selection of partners is important at this point because it grounds the process in a social comfort zone. Plus, when all is said and done, friendships create the substance for the most dynamic duos.

"Come to the rug, bring a partner, and sit down together. Then, hold your partner's hand up in the air, please," I invite. When everyone is ready I explain exactly what we are going to do and why we are doing it in that manner, which is actually what some call a think-aloud. In so doing, I walk the class through how I wonder about books as I read them. This will become their model to emulate.

"It's fun to wonder!" I say. "That's why authors write books. They *want* us to wonder."

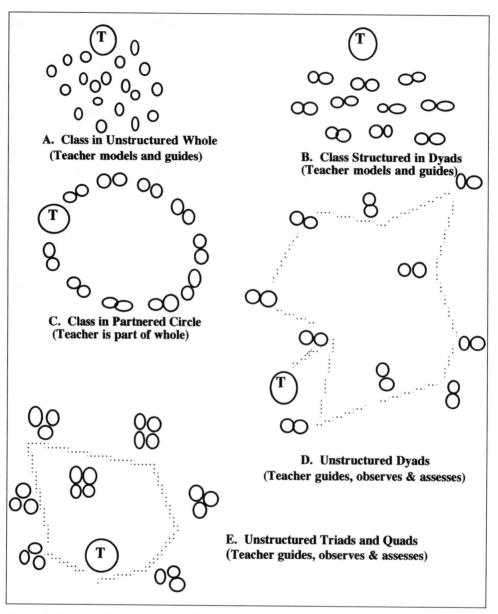

A. Class in Unstructured Whole
(Teacher models and guides)

B. Class Structured in Dyads
(Teacher models and guides)

C. Class in Partnered Circle
(Teacher is part of whole)

D. Unstructured Dyads
(Teacher guides, observes & assesses)

E. Unstructured Triads and Quads
(Teacher guides, observes & assesses)

Figure 2–1   Social Structures for Teacher-Student Interactions

We next reference our chart with its good conversation tips, reading it over one more time, just as a reminder. Then, I begin.

FROM WONDERING TO ITS RESPONSE

Modeling Wonders with a Tentative Response

I start the lesson with a brief introduction regarding author, title, and copyright date—and usually a short prereading introduction. After I've read about a page of text, I stop to offer my first wonder. That is, I wonder right out loud what I'm thinking about what I've just read. For instance, if I'm reading Van Allsburg's *Just a Dream*, after the first couple of pages, I might stop and respond, "I wonder why that boy threw his garbage all over the ground?"

I follow my first couple of wonders with a brief, tentative response that usually begins with the word *maybe* and includes *because*. I might say, "Maybe he doesn't care about keeping the ground clean because he doesn't realize what can happen." In so doing, I am demonstrating an important skill: how I add reasonable evidence to substantiate my conjectures.

More often than not, students feel compelled to offer responses to my initial wonders, so I use such comments to fuel the fires of the process. Before I move on, I celebrate the fact that wonders usually do provoke listeners to respond just as they have; when that happens, it is the beginning of conversation. I continue reading, wondering, and allowing the responses to my second or third wonders to unfold, extending those retorts even further; that is, I continually piggyback off each child's responses.

Teacher-Student Duos Demonstrate the Dynamic Process

Frequently, several students will simultaneously voice their thoughts. It's then that I select one as a partner, so that I can demonstrate how *they* will interact with *their* partner. That is, I try to create a minimodel where one teacher-student dyad bounces ideas off each other—and in the process becomes a dynamic duo. Kids need these minilessons that clearly demonstrate the conversation structure. This is an important feature in the process, because it lays a foundation that will be used again and again. Such demonstrations become their anchors to be emulated.

The photo at the beginning of this chapter shows how a student at Buffalo's International School and I modelled the knee-to-knee response pattern for others in the class. Accordingly, I usually get up and sit across from that student with whom I will be interacting. I try to keep the conversation going by offering honest responses to the student's thoughts; when the topic wanes, I offer up another

These first graders are caught up in text response with each other as they sit knee to knee.

related wonder to maintain the flow. I gesture repeatedly, just as adults do in real conversations. I nod, smile, and utter, "Uh-huh," all the while hoping that my partner will mirror my behaviors. Eventually, I move back into the book.

This, then, is how students learn to see themselves as text wonderers and responders. They simply model what they've observed. And it works—even with the youngest students.

It's important for the class to live through what will soon be expected of them and to articulate their related observations for our growing Conversation Tips chart. When students have observed a few of these minimodels, I tell the group that the next time I stop I'll be inviting *them* to turn to *their* partners, sitting knee to knee and eye to eye (see photo on page xxiii) to share wonders and responses. I find that every elementary classroom enjoys moving into the knee-to-knee structure—if for no other reason than the opportunity it provides to change seating position, that is, to fidget.

When a class has an odd number of students, a triad must replace one duo. These girls dedicatedly respond to the teacher's read-aloud of a Van Allsburg book.

What If Some Kids Don't Wonder?

For one reason or another, there always seems to be one or two dyads who do not fall into conversation once they are knee to knee. In such cases, I join that pair for a brief period and try to grease the wheels of progress by presenting them with obvious and specific text-related wonders. That is, if the story is *Little Red Riding Hood*, I might ask, "Don't you wonder why her mother is letting her go into the woods alone?" or "Don't you wonder why her mother isn't worried for her safety?" or "Don't you wonder why her mother is giving her wine to take to her grandmother?" I ask these questions in a way that infers, "Goodness! Everyone in the whole world must be wondering this!" It's difficult for students to be reticent when presented with such real wonders, so even the most complacent or shy dyads use this extra nudge to open their doors to response. Truly, it's never failed!

HONORING WONDERS WITH THE CLASS

After the dyads seem to be comfortably sharing and responding to each other, I work to scaffold them further using a follow-up, whole-group share. That is, partners are invited to share with the rest of the class what interesting wonders they had within their dyad. Usually, several are eager to bring their wonders into the whole-group context. But, to invite students to consider the importance of response, I usually refocus that volunteer on his partner, rather than on himself, by asking, "How did your *partner* respond when you presented that wonder to him?" Again, I am reinforcing a process that honors responses to wonders, as well as wonders themselves.

To carry it even a step further, I ask the whole group if anyone else has a response to that student's wonder, which I then reiterate. This honors students who lay their thoughts on the floor for others to contemplate, but it also tends to reveal commonalities in thinking among the group. Students often blurt out, "Hey, that's what I was wondering!"

CELEBRATING TENTATIVE RESPONSES

This is also a convenient time to draw attention to how many of their responses begin with "Maybe . . ." or "Probably . . ." or "It could/might be. . . ." I celebrate these tentative responses, these predictions, because they present a somewhat different school culture—one where *maybes* and *probablys* are as important as right answers. I like my students to feel that reasoned possibilities are always important—even though we may eventually discover their fallacy. The kids come to understand that in our classroom, both tentative and definitive responses have their place.

To further make my point, I like to expose a few of the maybes and possiblys that arose during the lives of the world's greatest thinkers, such as Einstein or Edison—the tentative hypotheses that were eventually realized (as well as some that were not). In other words, our goal here moves beyond cut-and-dry, right answers to what might be reasonable possibilities—ones that can be supported with evidence. Such hypotheses often include an explanatory "because" statement.

Even primary-age children can be prompted into using evidence. I merely ask them, "Why do you think that?" or "What has happened that makes you say that?" It takes but this small, guided nudge to move kids further into comprehension. Eventually, they learn to internalize that nudge.

Following are some examples of such tentative responses from kids who have no doubt internalized the process and are responding to *Toliver's Travels* again. Notice how some of them are already providing evidence to support their maybes or probablys.

Darien: *Probably* not because they're downstairs and sometimes when you're in bed you can only hear a murmur when someone's talking?

Asa: And, it's *probably* some time when they're not ending [the war], because if the red coats are in their house, then—

Lucia: She *might* even be an English spy or something.

Sim: That's a good point. I think *maybe* she's just having a hard time.

Asa: *Maybe* she's an orphan.

In another example, Amy Patterson's students were discussing Roald Dahl's *Matilda* when Tiana presented them with a wonder that sparked the following conversation:

Tiana: I wonder why they call the TV "the tellie."

Anna: [laughing] Yeah, really!

Ellie: *Probably* because they watch TV so much.

Jennie: Or, *maybe* they watch the show that's called *The TV Tellie*.

Ellie: Or, *maybe* they watch *Teletubbies* or something.

Jennie: I don't *think* they had *Teletubbies* back then.

Not Just Any Old Maybe

Sometimes, kids get the idea that words like *maybe* and *probably* are not school words. They think that schools are only right-answer places, where anything less is inappropriate. I help them understand that maybes and probablys are accepted and respected in my classroom and that "we can't be creative if we refuse to be confused" at least some of the time (Wheatley 2002, 33–34).

But, I also let them know that just any old maybe will not serve our purposes. Instead, maybes and probablys should always be *educated* guesses, which means each one needs to be based on *all existing known facts*. As a consequence, many of our "maybe" and "probably" responses will be followed by "because." I tell students this and go on to demonstrate it. For instance, "The county is probably going to start its renovation soon, *because* I saw a lot more equipment at the sides of the road today." I offered an educated guess to my question—"I wonder when they will begin road renovation?"—and supported it with some evidence.

Thus, we celebrate tentative responses, as long as they are not silly, but instead accompanied by reasonable evidence. Kids are in love with the word *because*, so this substantiation process is easier than it may appear. It is also an important oral rehearsal component that leads students into providing rich and related evidence for their written responses. They come to understand that any old answer is not good enough; there must indeed be evidence to back it.

GUIDED COMPREHENSION USING A STATEMENT-EVIDENCE CHART

Connecting answers to evidence is an important comprehension strategy. Students come to understand that their evidence can come from one or several places—the more the better. That is, evidence can come from their own experiences, from the experiences of others, from the text they are reading, or from other texts they have viewed, read, or heard. Chapter 4 investigates this process in greater depth.

A Statement-Evidence chart can offer young learners a more concrete form for making such connections. Using a double-entry (two-column) format, we can log student maybes on the left side, while placing the evidence for each on the right. For example, after reading *Jack and the Beanstalk*, the following Statement-Evidence chart might develop:

Statement-Evidence Chart		
IDEA	(because)	EVIDENCE
Maybe the giant deserved to be angry.		Jack broke his home. Jack stole his harp. The housekeeper was on Jack's side.

QUESTION AND RESPONSE DEPTH: THICK OR THIN?

There is a grand variety of interrogatives from which speakers can choose when they want to ask a question. I believe it's helpful to show students this variety of choices, invite them to discuss and list question differences, and then keep that list handy during question-response activities. I have developed such a list for quick and easy reference, and it can be used throughout the remainder of this chapter and in future lessons (see Figure 2–2).

Who is/isn't   What is
Who was/wasn't   What was
Who can/can't   What can
Who does/doesn't   What does
Who did/didn't   What did
Who will/won't   What will
Who might   What might
Who should   What should
Who could   What could

Where is   How is
Where was   How was
Where can   How can
Where does   How does
Where did   How did
Where will   How will
Where might   How might
Where should   How should
Where could   How could

When is   Which is/isn't
When was   Which was/wasn't
When can   Which can/can't
When does   Which does/doesn't
When did   Which did/didn't
When will   Which will/won't
When might   Which might
When should   Which should
When could   Which could

Why is/isn't   What if
Why was/wasn't   What makes
Why can/can't   What made
Why does/doesn't
Why did
Why will/won't
Why might
Why should
Why could

Figure 2–2   Interrogative Choices

Questions or ideas and their responses have a codependent relationship. That's why it's important for us to consider the opposite end of questions, that is, the responses that they evoke, because without a back-and-forth interaction pattern, there is no conversation. With this in mind, let's look first at question depth, which will in turn predict response depth.

As students crawl further into wondering, they come to realize (with the help of their teacher) that responses to "where" and "why" questions differ in depth. They learn that "where" questions are often answered by a quick reference to the text or a brief response. We could therefore call these (as well as "who" and "when" questions) *thin questions*. However, "why" as well as "how" and "if" questions generally call for some thought and in-depth searching and connecting, and are therefore dubbed *thick questions* (Harvey and Goudvis 2000).

Guided Comprehension Using Thin Questions and Their Responses

Furthermore, "where" (or thin) questions frequently evoke a literal response, whereas "why" (or thick) questions are rooted in inference. Literal responses are surface structure answers that can usually be located right there in the observable text and can easily be judged as correct or incorrect: Where? In the deep, dark woods. Where? In Northern Italy.

When used to discuss a piece of literature, these literal or surface structure questions do not usually generate interesting conversation because they have short, often uninteresting answers. These are the questions we often see in workbooks and on tests, because space for response is limited. When they do appear in conversations, they are usually evoked to breach a fact gap; that is, when the speaker is explaining something and has perhaps forgotten a character's name. Once he has that name, he is able to move on to the point he is trying to make.

However, when inference creeps into a thin question response, substantiation can thicken the results. For example, when Heidi Clarke's fourth graders were reading *Toliver's Travels*, Lucia asked a question that might well have been literal in nature on a workbook comprehension exercise. However, this seemingly literal question offered within the context of a conversation evoked a far more in-depth response than a workbook page would allow. Lucia's question and the ensuing interactions follow:

Lucia: Who is Dicey?

Asa: Maybe she's an orphan.

Sim:	It's on page, um-m-m. [*searching*] She just looks—she fits the description and her hair [*looking at a picture*] and all, I think she's having a hard time in her life.
Lucia:	She might even be an English spy or something.
Holly:	But, if she was she wouldn't be living with them.
Sim:	That's a good point. I think maybe she's just having a hard time.

This interaction lets us see how even a surface-level question within the context of a conversation can prompt kids to think deeply, to delve into every possible avenue that might help more comprehensively answer that seemingly simplistic question—in this case, "Who is Dicey?" What the students saw hidden within the literal here was "What does Dicey have to do with the story, how does she fit into the plot, why did she do what she did, and what motivated her to do it?" Responses such as this are expected far more often in conversations than on workbook pages or on tests. Yet, isn't this what comprehension is all about?

Guided Comprehension Using Thick Questions and Their Responses

On the other hand, some questions more obviously evoke a thick response—spoken or written. For example, "why" questions often call forth interesting, exciting, and sometimes debatable answers. Such questions involve more explanation, more details. They call to our deep structure, requiring us to crawl down between the lines, to revisit prior text and prior knowledge, to infer, to make subtle connections between what the text is saying and that which our own past experiences suggest. Sandra and Spayde (2001) point out that "why" questions usually lead to philosophical discussions, while "how" questions invite practical discussions and problem solving.

In the following we see a thick, rich response to a "why" question, as these fifth graders in Mikal Murray's class struggle with the death of a character. Throughout *Number the Stars* by Lois Lowry, this group of students struggled with many philosophical issues as they tried to come to grips with unconscionable acts.

Liz:	You know, I said [*checking her sticky note*] "Why did they kill Peter?" He's not Jewish.
Lois:	He was protecting everybody. He didn't *have* to be Jewish.
Liz:	I know, but you know how they said that he was protecting people, well wouldn't everyone else be killed too, along with him?

Mona: They captured him.

Liz: They only captured *him*?

Nigel: Because they found this confederation he was a part of, and so—

Liz: But I mean this happened before!

Mona: It was two years after this was.

Lois: Because he had written a letter. It was two years after. It said [*reading*], "He had written a letter to him on the night he was shot, and simply said that he loved them and that he was not afraid and that he was proud to have done what he could do for his country and for the sake of all the people." So, he had been helping the people out, and the Nazis found out—

Liz: So *that's* why!

Lois: Right, so he was helping people get—

Liz: Yeah, they just said that he was happy that he did that, but they didn't quite say why. They just said whether he got captured or not.

Nigel: They actually buried everybody they saw helping him do it.

Lois: It said, "He simply buried them when they were killed and marked the graves only with numbers." Obviously, there was more than just Peter.

Developing deep, rich answers for thick questions is an important skill that is needed to do well on school performance assessments, as well as in many real-life careers. When the supervisor asks a thick question, like "Why are sales down?" it's probably not wise to answer with a thin response, such as "People are not buying." That supervisor, no doubt, wants to know every single detail related to why sales are down, so that the company can in turn do something about it. "People are not buying" is an answer, but it is a gist or general answer. It is a surface structure answer. The boss wants the details to back it up. (Gist answers are further explained in my 2001 text *Better Answers: Written Performance That Looks Good and Sounds Smart*.)

GUIDED COMPREHENSION THAT DEVELOPS INFERENTIAL THINKING

It is easy to see how students who have continual experiences in literature conversations will grow the strategies for inferential reasoning. They'll come to understand that their peers will ask them for evidence to back their thinking, and they'll begin to search for and consider that evidence *prior to* the conversation itself, in order to be prepared. Primary students whose peers ask them to go back and search the text to prove a point will eventually internalize that sense of preparedness and come to the group ready, with evidence, to prove their points.

Working together, students come to realize that they must dig down between the lines to dredge out the subtleties and inferences that will support their hypotheses. They soon learn that inferences are the maybes and the probablys they conjecture, but those tentatives are of far less value without evidence to back them up. Thus, we must encourage the tentative hypotheses, for they represent the inferences; however, both teacher and classmates must also motivate students to substantiate such statements of probability with evidence. Again and again, we must ask, "Why do you think that?" and "Why do you say that?"

The Stranger, by Chris Van Allsburg, prompted many hypotheses in Denise Vassar's fourth grade at Buffalo's International School 45. I stopped reading to invite wonders after a section where the stranger helped the father work in the fields, and although the father was very tired, the stranger "did not even sweat."

These fourth graders back their hypotheses with evidence from the story. The child on the right ticks off each piece of evidence on her fingers as her partner actively listens.

Notice how Jose backs his wonder with two pieces of evidence, and then Dawan offers yet one more.

> *Jose:*   I wonder if he's a robot or something because he's *not sweating* and he's *doing all this work*.
>
> *Dawan:*   And, he *never gets tired*.
>
> Jose: I know. That's just *weird*.

ANALYTICAL, CRITICAL, AND EVALUATIVE RESPONSES: GUIDED COMPREHENSION USING THICK, RICH INTERROGATIVES

For a grand number of years educators have been coauthors of a regurgitation culture. Yet spitting back facts and information is the lowest performance level in comprehension. Realistically, sticking to facts and information makes for a pretty boring conversation. Even interpretation of those facts is only one step above regurgitation.

It takes far more than this to live fully—especially in a democracy. We want our kids to think deeply and make connections. We want them to analyze and evaluate their interpretations. We want them to take an educated stance on issues. Basically, we want them to understand the "why" behind the "what is."

With experience in thick wondering, we come to realize that some of these interrogatives nudge responders toward the higher levels of thinking and questioning. Many wonders that call for a critical response incorporate the interrogatives *how*, *will*, and *why*. How will she feel when she finds out her sister took her new dress? Will she be angry? Why would her sister do something like that? Steeping students in critical response opportunities nurtures mature readers who stretch beyond the text parameters and into the real world. Such readers consider carefully who has authored a piece, for what audience the piece written was, what evidence backs their biases, and what the underlying purpose of the piece of writing is. We need to demonstrate this for kids.

Creative responses are frequently evoked by combining the interrogatives *how*, *why*, *who*, *when*, and *where* with *could*, *should*, and *might*. For instance, "Why could . . . ?" or "Who might . . . ?" Another interrogative evoking a creative response is *what if*. Again, responders will stand on tentative ground, so they must therefore support their creative responses with legitimate and reasonable evidence. Such responses will, consequently, be some of the thickest. Again, we need to demonstrate this for our kids.

40

Consider this lengthy and interesting discussion that developed when a group of my first graders were trying to decide whether *Mr. Popper's Penguins* was fact or fiction. Creative responses abound in the following dialogue.

Chrystal:	How 'bout if we—let's write [*looking at front cover of book*] to Richard and Florence Ashwater [the authors] and see if—
Jennifer:	What if they're dead, and you can't write to them?
Kyla:	Oh, they *might* be dead.
Jennifer:	What if they died? Yeah, they might be dead.
Chrystal:	Yeah, but look-it. Listen to this [*turning to the copyright page again*]. Look at this, okay?
Kyla:	Oh, yeah, it says right here, "Copyright"!
Chrystal:	"Copyright renewed 1960 by Florence Atwater, Doris Atwater, and Carroll Atwater—"
Zach:	They're too old *now* [*with finality!*].
Kyla:	'60s? It says 1960s? Hm-m.
Chrystal:	Look at this. Listen to this: [*She reads the entire "All rights reserved . . ." information from the copyright page of the book.*]
Others:	[*All look at Chrystal questioningly. They seem to be trying to understand how the information she just read might impact the answer to the fact/fiction dilemma.*]
Chrystal:	So?
Jennifer:	Yeah, but, well, what're we gonna say if we write?
Chrystal:	Is *Mr. Popper's Penguins* a real story or not?
Kyla:	Why don't we write to him and ask him if it's a *true* story or not?
Chrystal:	Yeah, that is what I was trying to prove.
Jennifer:	Maybe—what if, what if his uncle or dad's Mr. Popper?
Kyla:	So, it would still be alright if it was—
Chrystal:	I'll go do it right now.
Michael:	Wait a minute! Wait a minute! We don't even know who this was wrote by.
Chrystal:	Yes, we do! Richard and Florence Atwater.
Jennifer:	Well, why can't we write it all together. That would make it more interesting.
Michael:	Yeah!

The students continued trying to come to grips with this problem, and in the end they decided that even if the authors were dead, the publishing company should know. Thus, they wrote to ask. Certainly a creative response to the comprehension of text.

Evaluative wonders often ask the responder to critically compare or contrast similar with dissimilar entities or characteristics. Evaluative wonders usually fall somewhere along a response spectrum of possibilities from positive to negative. For younger children, comparisons may often fall along a good-bad spectrum, that is, good or bad behavior, good or bad story, good or bad experience. Regardless, the responder would need to support his opinion with evidence, so that when a student offers, "I think she is mean [a negative behavior]," we would nudge him to explain by asking, "Why do you think that?"

Amy Patterson's second-grade group reading *Matilda* grappled over the behavior of Matilda's parents, critically evaluating them. The following transcription demonstrates this:

Tiana: I wonder why Matilda's parents are not glad that Matilda is so smart.

Ellie: All they care about is only their sons and their selves. They're very rude parents.

Anna: Yeah, because they only like the TV, and they don't wanta really—

Jennie: Yeah, and they only like older people.

Anna: They don't really want—all they want is to, like, watch TV and not do anything else.

Ellie: Yeah, but she does like reading—

Jennie: Every afternoon.

Tiana: And, they only have TV dinners.

These students all seem to agree that Matilda's parents care only about themselves. However, they do not stop with their hypotheses. Instead, they collaboratively offer ideas that support their evaluation. To do this, they go back into the text to develop a deeper, thicker response to the initial "why" question. Other students can learn from Amy's students. They can investigate this transcription and search for the evidence that these second graders offer. This will help them later when they begin to investigate their own evaluative responses.

We've just explored a number of interrogatives, some of which tend to evoke richer responses than others. Certainly, those that call for a critical, a creative, or an evaluative stance are some of the more interesting. Reminding kids of this helps. As a matter of fact, the transcriptions in the Appendix of this book provide even more examples they can investigate and discuss with your guidance.

Furthermore, minilessons related to various interrogatives provide useful background, not only for literature conversations but also for developing responses to high-stakes written performance assessments. Students who have had a broad palate of questioning experiences can better predict what is expected and how they should respond.

MODELING A VARIETY OF WONDERS

After students have had the initial experience with partner wonders, I try to incorporate that same structure into a variety of venues throughout the week and on into the year. That is, every time I invite a group into a listening situation, I use that same technique—and I usually do not change partners for at least three or four weeks (see the research of Roger and David Johnson and Edyth Holubec [1990], which supports this). Partnered response not only refines conversation but also encourages more focused listening, because every student comes to understand that he or she will be playing an active role in classroom events. Passive, nonresponsive listeners will become a concern of the past.

As the students become more skilled in this dyadic sharing, the teacher can move on to model specific, text-related wonders and their responses. With the previous information in mind, try modeling the following strategies.

MODELING A BROAD SELECTION OF WONDERS

- *Questioning a character's intent:* For example, "I wonder why Goldilocks thought it would be okay to break into someone else's house."
- *Questioning the author's intent:* For example, "I wonder why E. B. White selected a spider as the main character of *Charlotte's Web*."
- *Questioning the meaning of a word:* For example, "I wonder what supercalifragilisticexpialidocious really means."
- *Considering another point of view:* For example, "I wonder why no one stops to question Chicken Little."
- *Reflecting on the author's skill:* For example, "I wonder how J. K. Rowling thinks up all the fantasy for her stories."

- *Reflecting on the illustrations:* For example, "I wonder why they chose to use real photos in this book, rather than illustrations."
- *Hypothesizing or creating a new avenue of thought:* For example, "What if he had won the race? I wonder what would have happened then."
- *Comparing/contrasting with other literature/authors:* For example, "I wonder why Harry Potter books remind me of Roald Dahl books."
- *Evaluating the text:* For example, "I wonder why the author chose to end the book that way. It is such a downer."
- *Connecting one's own life to text:* For example, "I wonder if that author grew up in the mountains, too. This story reminds me of what I used to do in the mountains."

As time goes by, it is noticeable that both questions and answers become richer and more interesting in classrooms where students readily have opportunities to converse. This means that teachers who move oral transactions into all subject areas and throughout the day will reap the benefits.

MOVING WONDERS INTO OTHER SUBJECT AREAS

Rich questions or wonders evoke rich conversations across the curriculum. For instance, when a story problem or a tessellation is presented in math, the teacher can turn to the partnered group and ask, "What are you wondering? Share what you are wondering with your partner." When a historical video is being viewed, the teacher can press pause and ask, "What are you wondering? Share what you are wondering with your partner." By doing this, she changes a passive listening culture into one that is active and vibrant, critical and creative.

Eventually, "What do you wonder?" becomes catching, and unprompted, the students themselves begin asking each other, "What are you wondering?" This creates an atmosphere of inquiry, an environment where wonder is expected and respected. Furthermore, it is the connecting of hearts and minds—the sustenance of the scientist, the art of the anthropologist, and possibly even the hope for humanity, for the solving of problems always begins with a wonder. But, this only happens when we trust the kids.

ASSESSMENT: A BASIC RESPONSE CHECKLIST

When I used knee-to-knee protocols in my first-grade and multiage classrooms the students and I would develop a simple checklist that would keep us all focused in a positive direction. Furthermore, it encompassed far less time to run through a brief list than our growing list of observations.

Each day before we began a knee-to-knee experience, I would draw attention to the chart. Then when we were finished, we would read each guideline aloud, and I would ask students to signify if indeed they followed that specific guideline. Here is one of my first checklists, which I called Conversation Self-Evaluation.

Conversation Self-Evaluation Checklist
by Mrs. Cole's Class

_____ I listened to others in the group.

_____ I looked at the person speaking.

_____ I responded to many of those who spoke.

_____ I listened to someone who disagreed with me.

_____ I asked someone to explain if I didn't understand.

_____ I spoke so that all the kids could hear.

_____ I talked my fair share—not too much, not too little.

_____ I tried to include others.

_____ I was polite.

I thought my contribution today was:

_____ usual. _____ better than usual.

_____ less than usual.

My favorite thing about this conversation was _____.

Eventually, I made quarter-page copies of this checklist and occasionally asked kids to respond in writing, simulating all their oral rehearsal experiences.

CLASSROOMS IN ACTION: DYNAMIC DUOS

The children in Mrs. Ceprano's class had viewed a video demonstrating individuals involved in conversations, and they had created a long list of the positive behaviors they observed—behaviors that they, themselves, could model in order to develop their own rich and interesting conversations. So Mrs. Ceprano decided it was time to invite the class into a conversation experience of their own.

The teacher wanted the group's first experiences to be positive, so she chose one of Chris Van Allsburg's books to read. As she took *The Polar Express* off the shelf, she began to explain to the class what they were about to do. She invited them to keep the chart on conversation behaviors in mind as they found a partner and came to the community carpet in the back of the room.

Several students attempted to pick the same partners and after a brief period of minor confusion, everyone arrived, partner in tow. "For this activity, I would like you first to be sitting alongside your partner, but facing me. Eventually, you will be sharing with your partner. At that time you will turn and sit cross-legged; your knees should actually be touching those of your partner. Therefore, you will be knee to knee and eye to eye. So, if you are ready to begin, hold your partner's hand up in the air. Now, try moving quickly knee to knee with your partner." All students responded accordingly, so the teacher continued, "Okay! That's the key word for moving back alongside your partners, elbow to elbow" (as in Figure 2–1B).

"We are learning how to be involved in literature conversations in order to share our reading together in rich and meaningful ways. Eventually, we may even want to videotape some of our own conversations!" The students' delighted faces demonstrated their excitement about the videotaping idea.

"We'll be starting off with wonders," Mrs. Ceprano told the group. "Wonders can be anything at all that you wonder about as you read a book, view TV, listen, or watch. Using this book," she continued, holding *The Polar Express* up in the air, "I am going to show you how I wonder my way through text. First, I will do it, and then after I think you have the idea, I'll ask you to do it. Okay?" Everyone seemed eager to begin, except Jon, who excitedly inquired about being videotaped. The teacher responded by telling the class that they would have to work their way into the process before they could think about bringing a camera into the room. And then she began.

"*The Polar Express* . . . h-m-m-m. I wonder if this book has a setting in the Arctic or somewhere like that because it has *polar* in the title. By Chris Van Allsburg. I love his books because they make me wonder. Someone once called him the Stephen King of children's literature, and I agree; he makes everything seem mysterious. The copyright date is 1985, so this book is—h-m-m-m," wondered the teacher. Immediately, Jordan correctly did the math and called the book's age, after which Mrs. Ceprano turned to the first page, showed the class its corresponding picture, and then read it aloud. When she finished the page, her eyes moved upward to the ceiling in a pondering stance as she responded to what she had just read: "You know, this page keeps saying, 'I did this,' and 'I did that.' I wonder if Chris Van Allsburg, himself, really did have an experience like this, and now he is telling about it. Kind of like a memoir or an autobiography." She then quickly looked back to the book, turned the page, and began reading the next part.

When she finished, she looked at the group and said, "I wonder if he is just dreaming or if this is really happening. Maybe he is dreaming, because he *was* in bed." Several children began to offer their ideas, so the teacher moved over and across from Tony.

Tony excitedly responded, "It said 'late that night,' so he probably *was* just dreaming."

Respectfully, the teacher honored Tony's response and extended it. "I guess I didn't even remember that, Tony. That's a great observation! I also think maybe being in his PJs gives a clue, too. In fact, I think I've read other books where the whole story is a dream," she continued, connecting to other texts for evidence.

"Me, too," answered Tony. "Like *The Wizard of Oz*. Remember? Dorothy was dreaming, wasn't she?"

"I believe she was," said Mrs. Ceprano. "Let's read on and see if our prediction is on target."

"But first, let me just say that I loved the little conversation Tony and I just had. We went back and forth, and back and forth. That's exactly what happens in every good conversation," the teacher explained.

For two more pages Mrs. Ceprano continued in this manner, stopping to wonder and inviting responses to her wonders. She then told the group that the next time she stopped, they would have a chance to turn knee to knee and eye to eye with their partners to share wonders. "Let's remember though," she reminded, "every wonder deserves a response. And the best wonders start a back-and-forth conversation. That's what we're aiming for: a back-and-forth conversation."

Mrs. Ceprano read on, stopping after two pages and inviting the group, "Share with your partner what you are wondering." Although almost all of the students began responding in the expected fashion, the teacher noticed that Mohammed and Jacob were just sitting knee to knee without any interaction. So she approached them, knelt down, and asked, "What are you two wondering?"

"I don't know," Jacob muttered with a shrug.

"Nothin'," responded Mohammed.

"Do you know what is going to happen when they get to where they're going?" asked Mrs. Ceprano.

Both boys said they did not.

"Well then, that is what you must be wondering. Mohammed, why don't you wonder that to Jacob ?" encouraged the teacher.

So, without actually looking eye to eye with Jacob, Mohammed asked the question, and the teacher stayed long enough to encourage Jacob to respond. When Jacob said he thought the characters were going to Toyland, Mrs. Ceprano responded, "What do you think, Mohammed? Think that's where they're going?" Expecting the boys to continue, she walked back to her book to continue reading.

Mrs. Ceprano read a few more pages so that students could have more opportunities to share. Eventually, the teacher stopped the routine to issue an invitation for partners to share with the whole group what went on within their dyad. Hands went up, so the teacher called on Shallandra, who responded, "I wondered why Santa picked that kid. He coulda picked any one of those kids. But he picked that dreamer kid. Why?"

"And how did your partner respond to that wonder, Shallandra?" the teacher asked.

"He said maybe it was because that kid was the only one in pajamas," reiterated Shallandra, with a postcomment giggle.

"Anyone else have a response to Shallandra's wonder? Why do you think Santa picked that kid?" the teacher asked.

"But there were lots of kids in pajamas," Elsa interjected with her hand up. "Turn back, Mrs. Ceprano. Show them those other kids. Turn to that page with the train. Remember?"

So Mrs. Ceprano turned back and, sure enough, the others were wearing pajamas as well. She then added, "This is a great conversation. We are even going back to check and prove our points. I wish I had this on video! You're going to be having some great conversations, I can tell, because you are already doing lots of good things—like giving evidence to support your ideas."

"So maybe we can be videotaped tomorrow?" Jon again inquired.

Laughing, Mrs. Ceprano responded, "Friends, I think we have a performer in our midst. Patience is a virtue, Jon. We will get to the videotaping eventually, and you will definitely be a part of it!" Jon smiled, satisfied for the moment.

Mrs. Ceprano continued to read and invite partner responses, followed by one or two students sharing their partner interactions with the whole group while the teacher used every possible entry point to connect to the conversation behaviors that they had already logged on their chart. Then, after the book was finished, she asked, "Did anyone notice anything else that we did not have on the chart that might be another good thing to add?" Clyde raised his hand, so the teacher called on him.

"I noticed that we talked a lot more about the pictures, and on the video they didn't say much about pictures. Maybe they didn't even have pictures! I think it's good to talk about the pictures," offered Clyde.

"Well, what should we write, Clyde?" asked Mrs. Ceprano.

"M-m-m-m. Maybe we could write: 'Use the pictures to—uh, uh—help you figure things out,' " interjected SuLinn.

"Yeah," Clyde agreed.

"Sounds like a good one. Now, Clyde, why don't you get a colored marker and add that one to the list?" encouraged Mrs. Ceprano. And then she added, "Anyone else have a different idea?" But no one else had a suggestion, so the teacher culminated by reminding the group: "Continue using the things that worked for you today. And the next time we have a read-aloud, you'll have another opportunity like this to partner share. But this was a great beginning!"

PARTNERING, A PERFECT PLACE TO START

Partnering, through its easy wondering interactions, has laid the initial stepping stones that have helped us as we begin our journey into conversations. Both teachers and students usually feel good about this part of the process. It's easy and it's fun. Although Step 3 is not quite so easy, it is indeed important in that it helps students and teachers peer inside conversations that unfold within a whole-group circle. Each time we call the circle, we learn how to respond in a group—probably one of the most important of life's skills.

Chapter 3

CALLING THE CIRCLE

The circle contains a magical power that defies superficial boundaries. If we want to bring
peace between the races it is important to meet in small, interracial circles; to bring peace
between men and women we must create truthful circles containing both . . . Once you have
been in a conscious circle with someone a bond is created that will last if you only see each
other infrequently.

Cahill and Halpern, Ceremonial Circle (1992, 3)

From the beginning of recorded history, the circle has been a sacred symbol—a
symbol of unity. It permeates numerous cultures, both past and present. Consider
campfire circles of the cavemen, the quilting circles of the pioneers, gatherings of
families around dinner tables, prayer circles, board meetings.

It was in circle gatherings around campfires that mythology arose and story
planted its roots. Participants learned to listen, to reflect, to share. The circle structure helped teach man and woman how to be civilized. It taught them how to
consider the perspective of others, how to negotiate, and how to find their place
within a group.

TABLE TALK

Actually, the large circle conversation is not new to education, either. In the first
half of the twentieth century, philanthropist Edward Harkness and Lewis Perry,
then president of Phillips Exeter Academy, wanted to develop a different system
of education where a "middling" student would not get lost. They put their heads

together and what evolved was a roundtable method that they called *table talk*, after Martin Luther's dialogues.

Table talk has been so effective that it is still the principal mode of instruction used at Exeter, where all "teachers and students are committed to an ideal of active, participatory, student-centered learning which is teaching students not just a given course's content but the skills required to become their own and each other's teachers" (Phillips Exeter Academy 2002).

If table talk has been the primary instructional mode for more than a half-century in one of America's most prestigious private schools, its track record alone says something. Every Exeter class—biology, history, English, math—is experienced in a roundtable setting, where students do not raise their hands to speak. "It's a lot about patience and everything, and not cutting other people off," explains one student in the school's Web video. "You have to be able to communicate with people who aren't like you and have different problems."

WHOLE-GROUP CIRCLES: A SCHOOL EXPERIENCE

These circles of learning should not only be called at Exeter. We need similar circles of sharing within our schools, for there is much to be learned through such an experience. Therefore, in this third step, we will implement the whole-group circle as a structure for the sharing of literature.

It is indeed uplifting to discover what can evolve when circles become an integral feature in the culture of schools. They serve as a venue through which children learn ways to settle their differences, to find those who care about them, and, likewise, to develop a care and appreciation for others and their ideas.

Although calling the circle is a very important piece of the literature conversation puzzle, it is also the most difficult to implement. This is because we begin with a whole-group circle, that is, the entire class of students. In her book *Turning to One Another*, Margaret Wheatley (2002) helps us learn why circle conversations are difficult and even "messy."

> Because conversation is the natural way that humans think together, it is, like all life, messy. Life doesn't move in straight lines and neither does a good conversation. When a conversation begins, people always say things that don't connect. (32)

Thus, we have a whole class—maybe twenty-two students or so—all trying to participate in an optimal fashion. Not easy. Not easy at all. So, then, why move from the simplicity of the dyads in Chapter 2 directly into this large and complex structure? Why not implement smaller circles first?

Wheatley helps us begin to answer these questions, explaining that

> if we suppress the messiness at the beginning, it will find us later on, and then it will be disruptive. Meaningful conversations depend on our willingness to forget about the neat thoughts, clear categories, narrow roles. Messiness has its place. We need it anytime we want better thinking or richer relationships. (33)

So we can at least rest somewhat easier knowing that messiness is acceptable here, that better thinking and richer relationships will develop out of this mess. The remainder of this chapter explains other reasons for this complex, large-group structure, and it clearly substantiates the necessity of struggling through it. Just remember, it's downhill after that.

WHOLE-GROUP CIRCLES: A VENUE FOR ANCHORS

When students meet in dyads and small conversation groups, the teacher can work with only a few at one time, and each group's common experience differs from that of another group. However, when the entire class participates in a whole-group circle (see C in Figure 2–1), the teacher becomes a guide by the side of many at once. He also learns to use this platform to analyze and assess for instruction and to occasionally offer his own voice on a particular issue. Yet, the role of participant-observer is a sensitive one. He and the other participants must listen, observe, evaluate the process, and revise. Furthermore, the structure becomes a working model from which the class can develop *anchors*, that is, memorable aspects from circle conversations that can be used later as *reference models* (see Harvey and Goudvis 2000).

I remember one great anchor model that we created from a whole-group circle. That time, the conversation was shared between about ten kids, and it went back and forth among them for maybe five minutes or more. At any rate, it seemed like a very rich and involved set of meaningful and connected interactions. The kids were so proud of their responsive conversation that the whole class used it as an anchor, that is, a reference reminding others to dedicatedly engage in response so that their conversation would resemble "that time we were talking about ghosts."

The circle then becomes a whole-group shared experience from which we can gather new, in-process ideas to be added to our growing chart of what makes literature circles work well. What's more, metacognitive structures begin to take shape during circle experiences, for as we investigate the nuts and bolts of conversation, kids are learning how to talk about talk.

In Mikal Murray's fifth grade at Maplemere in Sweet Home, the kids were in circle listening to *My Side of the Mountain* when their teacher stopped reading to allow some conversation related to the part just read. We enter their discussion at a spot where they are struggling over the story's time frame.

Joey:	Yeah, it does. Yeah, it shows Rose when she's really old, and then it starts telling about the story and then like pieces of Rose comes back and tells more. And then it goes back to the movie and then Rose talks and then it goes back to the movie.
Samantha:	Well, the first chapter would be like it was just starting, so it's like any other chapter in the book. But *then* on page 112 it says, "Now I am almost to that snowstorm." So, that's the point where the snowstorm hits and then where—
Sean:	Yeah, we're *past* where the snowstorm already hit.

The group continued struggling with this issue, which later became a perfect anchor experience for foreshadowing, for that is what the author was using. Approaching a confusing literary term in this fashion makes it more concrete and connects it to a lived-through experience. For this reason, anchors or reference models are important guides that help direct kids through the conversation process; however, they can also nudge them into using comprehension strategies and a grand myriad of response avenues.

WHOLE-GROUP CIRCLES: A REAL CHALLENGE

Suzanne Miller and Sharon Legge (1999) explain that when students are with partners or in small discussion groups the teacher has "only a tiny role as a mediator when she [moves] sometimes from group to group. The major instructional forum for learning a narrative mode of thinking is whole-class discussions . . . they fill out a bigger picture of meaning or possibility for [the] group" (33). These large forums therefore hold an important capacity within the curricular structure.

However, the large-circle structure also raises the conversation level of difficulty. Just as it is usually easier to dance with one person than with many, so too is it easier to respond to one than to many. Each time a participant wishes to claim the floor in order to share a response or an idea, to piggyback or to support, he must move into that space with grace and finesse. This is an experience in which children *really* learn the difference between interrupting and piggybacking.

GETTING THE CIRCLE ROLLING

A New Teacher Role: Silence

I start our whole-group lesson by explaining what we'll be doing. I also caution the group that these first circle conversations will be a challenge for me, the teacher, because I will not allow myself to say anything. One of the most consistent stumbling blocks that occurs during first circle experiences involves the teacher. We teachers are used to keeping things moving in the classroom. We do not allow silence to lie in wait. If no one is responding, then *we* usually do. We can't resist filling that void. Instead, what we really need to do is to trust the kids.

I tell the kids this, hoping I can actually meet the challenge that my oath of silence creates. But quite honestly, I have never known a teacher who did not have a difficult time with whole-class circles—merely because it is so hard to stay mute. But, until the teacher allows the class autonomy, they will remain unable to do it without her. She either contributes to codependency, or she suffers through the confusion that leads to their group independency.

Therefore, I try to keep this in mind as we begin the circle experience. I call the group together with their partners at first, and when everyone is sitting in a tight circle, ready to start, I remind them once more of the charted behaviors, after which I introduce the book and read aloud a couple of pages. When I stop, I say nothing. I just sit and look around the circle, waiting for one of the kids to say something in response to my reading. If no one talks, I wait . . . and wait . . . and wait.

If no one responds I ask the kids to go knee to knee with their partners again. This usually greases the wheels of conversation enough so that when they turn back to the whole group, they are more apt to offer a wonder within the larger setting.

Most often, what happens is that one student will venture forth with a wonder, after which all eyes automatically move to me, the teacher. You see, students are so used to the teacher-student-teacher (TST) response model (Mehan 1979), that by force of habit they anticipate that the teacher will respond. However, the teacher should not respond (even gesturally), except to look around the group, waiting for someone else to honor the wonder that is still on the floor. This is the tough part, because almost every teacher I know—including me—has this burning desire to say something, to fill that silent void to respond to the wonder. But we cannot. We must wait, because our silence is interpreted as "I think what you have to say is more important than what I have to say." And in the end, the waiting pays off.

I only maintain that silence, however, until the group begins to demonstrate a natural conversational flow, at which time I too become an active participant. However, by then, it is often difficult to get a word in edgewise. It even feels a little strange to have relinquished my throne.

Sometimes we teachers continue to claim such a focus of attention that we must consider a tactic that forces the group's attention elsewhere. There have been classrooms in which students have continued to look at me instead of their classmates. In that situation I simply remove myself from the group and sit behind the circle. I usually explain that I'll sit behind them and take notes on all the positive things I see happening—more good guidelines for our growing chart. My absence usually tends to rectify the problem, but not always. And, when they've finished, the group can't wait to hear what I've written, the good news. Always only the good news.

Let's look at the mindful responsiveness of the students in Mikal Murray's fifth-grade circle while the teacher remains the silent observer. Mikal had called the circle many times over a two-month period, so the class engaged in complete response autonomy. Mikal said nothing during the intermittent conversation that took place at each stopping point in the *My Side of the Mountain* chapter.

The students in the following example are predicting what might happen between Sam, who has been existing independently in the mountains; his father, who might visit; and his new friend, Bando. This is one brief example of what happens when a teacher meets the challenge of silence.

Nadine:	I think his dad is gonna wonder who Bando is, and Bando's gonna like—
Joey:	I bet they're gonna become friends—
Amad:	What if there's, like, a fight?
Nadine:	So, he'll be like, "Oh, well I didn't want to, uh—"
Sean:	"Interfere with Bando, maybe—"

Nadine:	"Because now your dad's here and you haven't seen him in a long time. So, I'll just go now."
Said:	He hasn't seen Bando either.
Andy:	He hasn't seen his dad in, like, five months! Bando came in September. This is only December now. He hasn't seen his dad since May.
Roberto:	He has spent time with Bando. Just now.
Sean:	But he *left* in September.
Andy:	Yeah! But then he left in May, so—
Roberto:	I think that his father—
Andy:	[*side comment to Sean*] He hasn't seen his father for *longer*.
Sean:	Oh-h-h.
Samantha:	So that was four months *after* he left that Bando came, so that was four months that he hadn't seen his dad.

Notice how the students are now finishing each other's sentences, using tentative responses, using previously read facts to substantiate their points, making educated predictions, and allowing for multiple-student participation. This kind of community does not magically arise. Mikal, an astute first-year teacher, had nurtured the process and allowed the group time to grow. (I might add that several of the participating students had been at-risk students.)

Don't Raise Your Hand!

Remember the comment by the Exeter student who was describing table talk? One of the first things he offered was: "You don't raise your hand." For schoolchildren who have been conditioned into this hand-raising behavior since kindergarten, it becomes a difficult habit to break. Yet we all know that in real conversations, people do not raise their hands to speak.

However, during (at least) their first couple of experiences with whole-group circles, students will continually try to raise their hands to add a comment. Usually, it is a fruitless endeavor, yet occasionally a classmate, recognizing the futility of the act, will actually give in to it and call on that person—in a manner that is all too familiar. Eventually, everyone comes to the understanding that, in order to speak in a whole-class circle, one must learn to dance in carefully, with grace and finesse.

Yet, sometimes a perceptive classmate will notice the intentions of a peer who is trying to enter the conversation floor, and that empathetic classmate may create a pathway for entry, just as Allie does when the whole group in Mikal Murray's fifth grade discusses *My Side of the Mountain* in the following dialogue. Agatha has been trying to break in to redirect the course of the group's predictions, because the others have forgotten a major factor, which Agatha is trying to share.

Agatha: But, going back—

Joey: Well, I think—

Allie: Agatha is trying to say something, you guys.

Agatha: But, going back to what Andy said, the Gribleys aren't very nature people, so here we are going on and on about they're gonna live in the forest, and they're not going to.

A little different twist to peer support came later during the same conversation. Note the timing of the teacher on this one.

Juan: Nigel would like to say something.

Samantha: And Mora hasn't said much.

Allie: She's tried, but everybody keeps interrupting her.

Nadine: Okay, let's hear what she has to say.

Mora: Well, now I've forgot.

Nadine: Just think about it for a minute.

Teacher: Think about it while I read some more.

It's fascinating to observe each unique dance of voices and gestures—far different from traditional classroom interactions. That is, I notice that in teacher-centered situations, students appear somewhat disengaged; they sit back, and occasionally a few students raise their hands and waggle their fingers, looking at the teacher—in a most predictable TST fashion. However, once they come to understand the unpredictable, interactive nature of the conversation process, they lean forward, concentrate on each speaker, and wait patiently, anticipating a segue when they can weave their own thread into the ongoing and evolving talk tapestry.

"Wonderitus! Wonderitus!" An Initial Glitch

Another initial glitch occurs when students get "wonderitus." They love the nomenclature I use for this syndrome that occurs when one child after another presents a wonder, but no one responds to any of the wonders. This is a very common occurrence that I do not interrupt to amend, because *after* the conversation, the issue can be brought forth during an assessment of how our conversation functioned that day.

When wonderitus first occurs, children appear quite pleased, because it is contagious and within a few minutes many children will have contributed. To the novice, the conversation will appear vibrant and alive, for many are contributing and things are moving right along. Yet if we later draw the students' attention to that period of continual wonders, which had no responses, they then realize that responding to a wonder with a wonder does not usually lend to optimal conversation—unless it extends the initial wonder, which indeed some do. The guiding principle remains: every wonder deserves a response. This becomes our ongoing mantra.

Even so, the beginning is very bumpy, and most often the group falls prey to wonderitus. Sometimes the kids themselves notice the syndrome and impulsively tell the group. That is what occurred during our first circle in Maria Fasolino's room at the International School in Buffalo. The students were listening to *The Witch's Broom* by Chris Van Allsburg when the following took place.

Mantia: The broom is probably cursed.

Lonnie: Uh-huh.

Mantia: I wonder if that's a witch.

Lucia: I wonder if it's power's back.

Roul: Wonderitus! Wonderitus!

Teacher: [*laughing*] It's hard, isn't it? It's a lot easier when you're with your partner, isn't it?

Class: Yeah!

Teacher: You'll catch on. Well, let's go on.

Alas, that was not the case, because after the teacher read the next section and stopped for conversation, many began saying "I wonder this" and "I wonder that." So, again, a student shouted, "Wonderitus!" Yet what a great anchor lesson this presented! It became an ongoing reference for offering a respectful response to others, instead of a self-focused wonder.

Circle conversations take time. They take patience. And, we all eventually learn, just like those at Exeter: "It's a team game right from the get-go" (Phillips Exeter Academy 2002).

Transforming Limelighters into Observers

Whole-class literature circles are difficult to implement for another reason. That is, there will always be a few students who love the limelight and continue to claim it, even when charted conversation tips are discussed beforehand. Yet, I tend not to identify these excessive behaviors as negative, because what we really *do* want is for everyone to be as excited and responsive as those few are. Consequently, I develop venues that shape overzealous floor stealing into forms that enhance, rather than deter, process. One of these involves a new responsibility.

To give others a chance to have a quality conversation without the constant voices of those overzealous few, I select about five or six students (and not all of them should be the overresponding individuals) to act as observers. Up to this point, only the teacher has assumed that responsibility.

A second grader takes notes as he observes his group in conversation.

First, I give each a clipboard and ask that all observers consider the charted behaviors and jot notes about the good things they see happening while their classmates are engaged in the conversation circle, just as they've seen me doing. Next, I ask each of the six to find an observation station behind the circle, so that during our literature conversation they can consider all positive behaviors and record those observations on a piece of paper. Theirs is a silent, writing role, which helps them (most of the time) develop listening skills without reprimands or repression.

Later, they do have their period in the limelight, for they are asked to report their positive observations to the group. This is a far more constructive reaction to overresponsive students. It will also re-create the social structure, allowing response space for other, less conversant students. It doesn't completely solve limelighter's syndrome immediately, because we can't ask those same kids to be observers every single day. But over time, they do learn the joy of listening.

ASSESSMENT: THE FOUR-FINGER ASSESSMENT RUBRIC

Creating a Four-Point Scale
Even after experiencing the observer role, a few students may continue to steal the show. That is, they focus only on talking, rather than responding. They do not understand the interactive nature of a conversation. To help kids develop a greater awareness of this limelighting tendency and to instill metacognitive conversation process behaviors in all students, I use a postconversation group assessment. This has turned out to be a most useful tool, yet it is a very simplistic little scale requiring little fuss or muss.

After the group becomes somewhat competent in large-circle conversations, I suggest we assess our success so far. I invite the group to help me develop some descriptors around a four-point rubric scale through which we can examine that day's conversation. (Rubrics are descriptions of a process—in this case, literature conversation—that are divided into categories and then performance levels.) I try not to spend a great deal of time on this, just enough to cocreate an easy-to-interpret scale with the class. I, the teacher, often have far more input than the kids at this point.

First, we skim the current Conversation Tips chart, searching for the most important descriptors. Next, we extract those that contain levels. For example, listening is important and it can be described through developmental levels, such as everyone listened, some listened, only a few listened, and so forth. After lots of discussion and revision, we come up with a satisfactory rubric that everyone understands. (This chapter's "Classrooms in Action" sections will provide more background on this process.) Regardless of the quality of the rubric, the most important aspect is that the students, themselves, are coauthors in the process.

Usually the rubric evolves into a form similar to the one that follows. Notice that descriptors are always stated in a positive form. I have never done two rubrics alike, but they often have similar attributes. For instance, on this one the first item deals with general physical behaviors, the second with the content discussed, the third with manners or gestures toward others, and the last ("Ready to be videotaped") is a special one I always try to fit into the lot. Although the kids get a kick out of the videotaping descriptors, they really do serve as delineators separating "pretty good" from "wonderful." After all, no one likes to appear any less than perfect when in front of the camera!

When developing an easy-to-use rubric, there is not only a sense of general categorical descriptors for each score, but gradations are also apparent, as can be evidenced on the following rubric. It becomes evident that descriptors often move in gradations from *all* to *most* to *some* to *few*. Even very young kids catch on to this concept. That is, moving from 4 to 1, notice how each score demonstrates a lessening of the skill, and although some descriptors connote negativity, all are stated in a positive form, which is often the most difficult part in the process.

A Four-Point Assessment Rubric Example

4 =   Everyone listened and responded.
We stayed on the topic and had interesting responses.
We invited others in and most kids had a chance to talk.
We were so great that we are ready to be videotaped.

3 =   Everyone tried to listen and many kids responded.
We stayed on the topic most of the time and had some interesting responses.
Several people had a chance to talk.
We will soon be ready to videotape.

2 =   Many kids listened and a few responded.
We strayed off topic sometimes.
Some kids had a chance to talk.
We need lots of work before we videotape.

        1 =   It was often hard to follow the conversation.
                  We skipped from topic to topic.
                  Only a few kids talked.
                  Hide the camcorder!

Using the Scale

After each point on the rubric scale is complete, I call the circle and ask all students to put up the appropriate number of fingers (the score) that defines our progress as demonstrated in that day's circle conversation. I wait until everyone has his assessment demonstrated using the finger code, and then I ask a few students with differing responses why they selected that particular assessment level. In other words, I ask each to use the rubric to explain what occurred during the conversation that can provide evidence to support that particular score.

For example, I might ask, "Libby, why did you give our circle conversation a 2 today?" And Libby might respond, "I gave it a 2 because mostly the same people talked the whole time." Libby's assessment falls right in line with the third descriptor under the score of 2. I might then lead Libby on into further explanation by asking her, "What does it look like when only some kids have a chance to talk?" And she might reply, "Some kids didn't listen."

At this point, I also remind the class not to mention anyone's name or target any particular individual. If the shoe fits certain individuals, they do eventually put it on! But, we try not to point fingers.

Even so, we need to move away from generalities and into specifics in order to refine our behaviors. So, Libby's explanation that "some kids didn't listen" is not specific enough. Yet how can we be specific without mentioning names? We can, because we instead describe only behaviors with no names attached. In so doing, the focus is on the behaviors, not the child. And, we need to tell exactly what *did* happen. For instance, we might say, "Some kids were bothering the person next to them by trying to take their spots." Or we could say, "Some kids seemed to be daydreaming and looking around the room instead of looking at the person speaking." It's important to articulate such behaviors because it helps students understand what *will* make the conversations work well. And, the more we refine, the more our chart grows—and the better we become at the process.

An example of a class-constructed rubric appears in the photo on page 63. Consider the ways in which this class and their teacher constructed the levels.

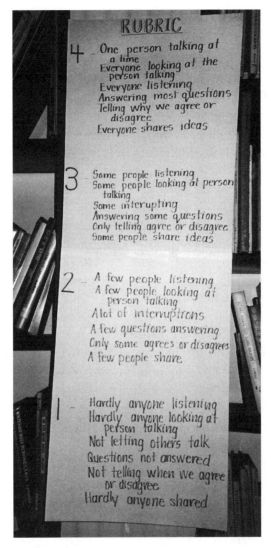

An example of a rubric scale in its final form

ANALYTICAL, CRITICAL, AND EVALUATIVE RESPONSES: GUIDED COMPREHENSION USING AN EVIDENCE-BASED PROTOCOL

By this point in the process the students will have observed multiple questioning possibilities, along with a variety of responses. Using the rubric on pages 61–62 on a regular basis will encourage them to monitor themselves and others while in conversation. Even very young students can do this. However, eventually we want to show students how to stay on the topic longer and make connections to relevant points.

Evidence-Based Terms

We can do this by modeling some evidence-based terms, ones that will crop up again and again if a responder has evidence for his or her statement. It is helpful to first display a chart with the following evidence-based terms on it:

- ◆ because
- ◆ for instance
- ◆ for example
- ◆ let me explain
- ◆ the author said
- ◆ earlier it said on page ___
- ◆ from our reading we know that

These terms are not always used when evidence is provided, but they are a good way to begin, especially with younger children. I would start by stressing *because* in kindergarten, for its connection to *why* was probably overlearned during their preschool "why stage." For instance, as three-year-old Delanie listened to Grandma read the last page of *Whose Mouse Are You?* by Jose Aruega, she noticed that another character had been added, a tiny baby mouse who was said to be "brand new."

"Why's *he* there?" Delanie asked.

"Because he's brand new," responded Grandma. "That's his new little brother. Like you're gonna have a new baby, too. Will you have a baby brother?"

"No-o-o! I have Mackenzie," added Delanie, making the connection between the text and her own life.

"Then you'll have a brand-new sister, like he has a brand-new brother," Grandma responded, helping solidify the connection.

The classroom transcripts in the Appendix of this book can be duplicated onto a transparency so students can actually search for evidence-based responses. I've included a couple here. The first one is a dialogue between some girls in June Peczkowski's fifth grade who are caught up in a dilemma over whether they want (the great) Gillie Hopkins to go to see her mother, who has put her into foster care.

Shanna: I want to her to go and then I don't want her to go. I mean I—

Mary: We all don't want her to go *because* she'd be safe with Trotter, and we want her to go *because* she might get to see her mother, but she probably's not wanting Gillie again, *because* she probably don't want her there, *because* if she abandoned her once, why won't she abandon her again?

The next example is from a group of second graders in Amy Patterson's class who are debating the wealth of the family in *Matilda*.

Delanie: Yeah, *'cause* they're rich and stuff.

Anna: Well, they're not really rich, or anything. They just care about themselves.

Ellie: Well, they are kinda rich *because* his dad gets a lot of money from the cars and stuff.

Delanie: Yeah.

Anna: Yeah, like two hundred dollars!

Jennie: [*emphatically with a touch of derisiveness*] *Because* he cheats.

Girls: Yeah!

Prompting Shallow Responders

Prompting shallow responders will help move them into providing evidence. Eventually, the kids themselves will begin using prompts, but they will need lots of experience to implement such devices in a natural manner. Above all, we do not want to create robotic-sounding responders.

PROMPTS FOR SHALLOW RESPONDERS

- ◆ Can you explain why you think that?
- ◆ What makes you think that?
- ◆ Why do you say that?
- ◆ How can you explain that?
- ◆ Would you please give us evidence for that idea?
- ◆ What facts do we know that support your thinking?

ASSESSMENT: POSTCONVERSATION PROMPTS FOR EVIDENCE

To introduce kids to evidence-based thinking, teacher Barb McKay offers an invitation after circle conversations. Her class had been studying Native Americans, but they were also investigating levels of friendship. A chart on the wall displayed several friendship levels, ranging from "awkward acquaintances" to "bonded brothers." When the large-circle discussion was over, Barb offered a specific reading-related question, which she asked her students to answer. But, notice what else Barb suggested: "What level of friendship do you think the two boys are at? Mark that level on a sticky note, and then go back into the book and back it with *why*. Mark that spot in the book with your sticky note, and be ready to share your thinking."

This kind of postconversation, evidence-based task can become a rehearsal for written performance. When a test question evokes an extended response, students come to understand that they must go back into the text to provide evidence for their thinking. Discussion helps pave the way to better written performance.

REHEARSAL FOR WRITTEN PERFORMANCE ASSESSMENT

I know that spoken rehearsal for writing helps because I, myself, presented a gazillion (rehearsal) workshops related to literature conversations *before* I wrote to Lois Bridges, the editor at Heinemann. It therefore makes sense that if kids live through discussion experiences, such as providing evidence for a statement, it will pave the way into better written response behaviors. This is the substance of guided comprehension.

Whereas if kids never grapple with ideas in a peer group, if they are never asked, "What makes you think that?" or if they have not made consistent connections between *why* and *because*, their written performance will lag behind those who do have such experiences.

Actually, providing evidence is a necessary real-world skill. That is, when the boss asks for an explanation for the decrease in sales, he will want evidence; when a product is faulty and needs to be returned, the letter should contain evidence of the object's faultiness; and when we apply for that perfect job, more than likely we will have to use evidence to show that we deserve it. Yes, these are important life skills that students are learning in literature conversations, and they are worth every inch of effort we put into the process. So, trust the kids and keep going!

Students in Barb McKay's class focus on a peer who has the floor for a moment.

CLASSROOMS IN ACTION: CALLING THE CIRCLE

Before school started on Monday, Mrs. Singh made sure that the edges of the area rug were free of obstacles. She was excited to move her students on to the next step in literature conversations, but she was apprehensive, too. She remembered last year when it took her class three weeks to become skilled in whole-group circles. Yet it had paid off, because after that, the process worked like a charm.

Later that morning, Mrs. Singh walked to the area rug and began to explain to the class the next step in the conversation process. "I'll be reading Chapter 2 of *The Chocolate Touch* to you today, but instead of talking with a partner, I'd like both of you to gather on the carpet with the rest of us in one large circle. Sit around the edges, cross-legged, so that we have a nice, tight circle. Then we'll discuss what we're going to do next." The students found their spots, each a part of the class circle, which also included the teacher.

Mrs. Singh then went on, "Today, as I read, stopping here and there for your responses, you will not be sharing with your partner. Instead, we will be sharing within this large circle. For the first few sessions, I'll be sitting in the circle with you, but I plan not to talk. I'll just leave the talking up to you for awhile. Now, this will not be easy at first—for me or for you—because there are twenty-three of us. That means we'll have to remember what makes conversations work well, and carefully follow those guidelines. Why don't we take a minute right now to skim the tips chart again?" The teacher then turned to the descriptors hanging behind her and, along with the class, skimmed through it quickly.

After a few minutes she returned to her plan: "I'll begin reading and when I stop, you may respond. Please don't wait for me to call on anyone or to be the leader. And there is no need to raise your hand, because we all know that people in conversation do not raise their hands to talk. Let's just talk about the story in the same way that we did with a partner, and then let's respond to anyone who offers something to the group. Remember: we need to honor every wonder with at least one response. Here we go. . . ." At that point the teacher began reading the book.

Mrs. Singh read the first two pages of the chapter and then stopped, turned the opened book upside down on the floor, and waited. The children looked around at each other, not certain of what they should be doing. Eventually, Thurston offered, "I wonder what that coin was all about—like, where did it come from?"

Everyone immediately looked at the teacher. But Mrs. Singh remained silent and looked around the circle, hoping that the students would get the idea that she was not going to respond this time. Tony filled the void by also turning to Mrs. Singh and responding, "That coin had John's initials on it. Maybe someone put it there for him to find." Mrs. Singh couldn't contain her smile, but she said nothing.

So Jennie added, "The book said that he goes over to Susan's every day along that path. Maybe someone did plant the coin there for him. Or maybe it was put there by some mysterious magician or something." Then Jennie's eyes also sought out her teacher, and they lingered there, waiting for her response.

Instead of accommodating Jennie's imploring gaze, Mrs. Singh turned to the next page in the chapter and began reading. She read a few more pages and stopped again. This time several children tried to begin at once. But Thurston, who was somewhat more confident, talked over the others and gained the floor again. As soon as he finished with his wonder, Heather offered another wonder. Then Carolyn entered quickly to share her wonder with the group. Eventually, Jennie responded to Heather's wonder, but the group was somewhat confused by then, because students weren't sure whether they should be wondering or responding to a wonder. And, if they were supposed to be responding, to whom should they respond when there were several wonders on the floor?

But, fortunately, Brad picked up on Jennie's cue and added his perspective. Then Carolyn piggybacked by agreeing with Brad. At that point the teacher returned to the book and began reading again. The group seemed to be gaining more understanding of how whole-group literature circles functioned. This became even more evident when the teacher stopped again for responses, because the circle's members were able to maintain a back-and-forth response pattern several times during that particular chat period.

When Mrs. Singh finished the chapter and the group experienced their final wonders and responses, she asked them to think about what went well with their whole-group conversation. "Let's develop a four-point rubric to assess our progress. If we think a conversation is a Level 4, it would have to be pretty terrific. We'd be ready to have someone come in and videotape us. We'd be ready to model for others. How would *you* describe a Level 4? Check our chart for tips."

The group offered a few suggestions, and Mrs. Singh scribed their thoughts, as well as her own, under the heading "Level 4." Then she moved on to Level 3. "I figure that at a Level 3 we would really be trying, but maybe running into some difficulty here and there. What do you think?"

The group worked their way through Levels 3, 2, and 1. Then Mrs. Singh asked them each to again consider that day's conversation. "I would like for all of you to raise your hands holding up the number of fingers that would represent the level of today's conversation."

Hands went up at various times until eventually all were displaying an assessment level. Mrs. Singh turned to Jacob, who was holding up one finger, and asked, "Jacob, why do you think we functioned at a Level 1 today?"

"Because we were lousy," responded Jacob.

"How's that?" nudged the teacher. "Look at the chart, please, and share with us what we did that puts us at a Level 1." (Notice that the teacher did *not* ask, "What did we do wrong?")

Jacob looked at the chart and said, "The same people talked all the time."

The teacher then turned to another child and asked why he felt the group performed at a Level 4. After this student gave his reasoning, Mrs. Singh said, "Well, it looks like most of us think we were either at a Level 2 or Level 3. Who would like to share some reasons for those assessments?" Again, students offered their thoughts regarding how closely the group aligned with the behaviors listed in the conversation tips or those listed in the notes Mrs. Singh had taken for each rubric point.

Mrs. Singh, herself, offered no final statement regarding the level at which the group had functioned. She knew this was only the beginning of the assessment process, so she did not use it as a platform for debate. She also knew that, given enough experience, most students would become adept at assessing conversations. They'd certainly have plenty of practice before the year was over. But she was pleased that the first whole-group circle had functioned so well, and she knew that the next one would be even better.

ALL GOOD THINGS TAKE TIME

Involving students in whole-group literature circles for a week may not be enough time to optimally develop the process. Most teachers find it takes longer—sometimes even a month. Once students are able to sit in the large circle and keep a rich, responsive conversation going (without the help of their teacher), it is then time to move on to the next step, where in a far smaller community, they will have more autonomy and a greater chance to respond. Calling the circle has prepared them for such independence.

Chapter 4

SMALL-GROUP RESPONSE
AFTER TEACHER
READ-ALOUDS

In this age of fast-paced lives driven into a frenzy by "surround sound" and ubiquitous telecommunications, the presence of book groups provides positive reassurance of the value of human discourse and affords a place where the imagination is free to explore.
Rachel Jacobsohn, The Reading Group Handbook (1998, 5)

With the most difficult part behind, we move on to small-group response to whole-group teacher read-alouds. It may be comforting to hear that this stage usually flows more smoothly. For one thing, by this point, students have had lots of experience sharing and responding, both with a partner and within a large group. Nevertheless, they have had the teacher right there to oversee each experience, and although we would hope that the teacher relinquished the floor to the students, his mere presence probably had an effect on student response and behavior. Unlike the previous step, this one is rooted in student autonomy; that is, students are weaned off teacher support during their conversations. The time has come for them to go it alone.

By now, students have come to understand that conversations are spontaneous and unrehearsed. They are not governed by teacher questions, nor do students have particular roles to play. They interact in no particular pattern; that is, like in real-life conversations, the participation is somewhat unpredictable. Obviously, the more loquacious speak frequently while quieter students sometimes need to be invited in. But by and large, there is a steady movement of talk among and between all members of the group in no predictable order.

DEVELOPING TRIADIC SOCIAL STRUCTURES

Don't Rush It!

Some teachers like to rush the process by attempting to move into small autonomous groups too quickly. After a few weeks of partner and circle conversation, teachers find it tempting indeed to skip the read-aloud and move into Step 5. That is, they try to incorporate postreading triads into their existing guided reading groups or SSR periods—times when the students themselves are responsible for the reading. But omitting the large-group read-aloud step courts difficulty. For one thing, the students have not actually worked in the triadic structure before. Nor have they been required to prepare for conversations by reading their own material independently. The strategies and tools in this chapter will sustain and enrich the more independent approach of Chapter 5.

Implementing this brief step guarantees greater success when students are invited into autonomous groups. Scaffolding behaviors introduced here become the foundation that will support students later on. For this reason, we do not as yet require the students themselves to read, but instead, the focus of this step remains on careful listening and rich responses.

The Stability of Triads

Roger and David Johnson and Edythe Holubec (1990), longstanding gurus in cooperative learning, suggest that three is the optimal number for collaborative groups. A group of three forms a triad; when members sit cross-legged so that each one's knees touch the person on both the left and on the right, this small group forms the most stable geometric form, a triangle. Other than partners, this is the only structure in which participants can face all members. That is one of the reasons triads add stability to a conversation setting. Yet, sometimes it may be necessary to have one or two quads (groups of four) because of total class numbers. It is recommended, however, that the primary structure be confined to three, with no dyads and as few quads as absolutely necessary.

Establishing Group Membership

Prior to implementing Step 4, the teacher should carefully group the class into triads. Each threesome should be as diverse as possible, and students should remain in that particular triad for at least two to three weeks. Again, the Johnsons and Holubec (1990) explain that it is best to keep groups intact for a few weeks so that members become comfortable with each other. This is just as true for adults as it is for children. Obviously, grouping errors do occur, in which case adjustments would need to be made.

Students should be told the members of their triad before the lesson begins, and the structure itself should be explained. I tell students that the triangle is the most stable form on earth and that it will therefore serve *our* purposes well. I explain how the group should sit, and then I ask three student volunteers to demonstrate how that structure will look. Obviously, girls with short skirts on will have to revise their sitting pattern. Likewise, older students, who may be expected to sit in chairs, can have the corners of their chairs almost touching. Regardless, this triadic form is important because it knits the group into a responsive whole.

Students in Leigh-Ann Hildreth's first grade interact after taking notes during their teacher's read-aloud.

USING MNEMONICS

A fundamental practice introduced early in this step involves the use of mnemonics, which come in many forms and are used to remind the reader or listener what he wants to say when he meets with his conversation group. Yet all students should use just enough words or symbols to jog the memory, because mnemonics are not meant to be read verbatim. I tell the kids that these tiny notes are just reminders.

Kinds of Mnemonics

Many of us who belong to book clubs write in the margins of our books in order to remember something important or to list points we want to make. Harvey and Goudvis (2000) call this "leaving tracks," that is, we leave a trail that we can go back and follow as a reminder. However, in a school setting, books do not usually belong to the students; consequently, they are unable to leave written tracks in the margins. Therefore, teachers use a variety of alternatives:

- sticky notes stuck to the appropriate page
- journal entries containing comments and their referenced pages
- blank bookmarks on which students can leave tracks or mark the spot

Kids seem to favor stickies. Such little notes are the most useful to me, too, because they enable me to mark the exact spot for easy reference. They therefore become the closest mnemonic to writing right on the page itself. Students like to leave a bit of the sticky note showing over the outside edge of the page, so they can easily turn to the referenced spot. I model all of these ideas to offer students choices.

It's important that students allow these little notes to serve their intended purpose; that is, sticky note messages should carry an at-a-glance reminder. They are not mini-epistles. One quick glance at a word or two—or even a picture or graphic—should jog a memory into action. As a matter of fact, it is actually best if we remember what we wanted to say *without even looking* at the tracks we've left.

Keep Mnemonics Brief

Teachers who use postreading literature logs, in which students are asked to write lengthy entries to the teacher or blackline master prompts, will not have as much success if they try to incorporate such responses into literature conversations.

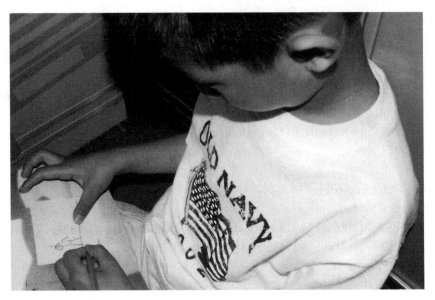

A young child leaves tracks using pictures.

Students' lengthy responses will take the spontaneity out of conversations. So, although elaborate spoken explanations during conversations can be apropos, the reading of essay responses is not—nor, for that matter, would essays be a part of adult book talks.

That is not to say that teachers should never ask a student to write a comprehensive postreading response. There's a time and a place for everything, and essay response writing serves a different purpose. (See my *Better Answers: Written Performance That Looks Good and Sounds Smart* [2001] for tips on written response essays.)

MODELING NOTETAKING DURING THE READ-ALOUD

Getting Ready

To begin, ask the class to move to the meeting area with a pencil and a clipboard or some object with a hard surface, such as a book, on which they can write. Students may sit either randomly or in a large circle (see A and C of Figure 2–1). The teacher should get ready to read aloud and model how to take mnemonic notes; that is, he will stop after every few paragraphs, or whenever it seems reasonable, to jot a reminder on a sticky note. Eventually, ownership in this process will be passed on to the students, just as it was in the previous steps.

Obviously, at this point, students will not be able to post their notes on the book's page, for (most of the time) the teacher is the only one with the book. But the use of stickies themselves is motivating. Plus, it helps kids transition into the expected behavior once they do have their own books. Some schools are fortunate enough to have class sets of particular books. In that case, students might have their own copy of the book that the teacher is reading and would therefore be able to place a sticky note in the appropriate spot in the text.

Likewise, when a reading series is the district mandate, their multiple copies also allow for this. It won't hurt, if for a day or two, the guided reading story in the reading series is read aloud to the students. This fits right into a shared reading situation, as well; that is, as the teacher reads aloud, the students can follow along in their own books, and when the teacher stops, the students can place stickies in selected spots, jotting a brief mnemonic on each—after the process is modeled.

Leaving Tracks: Guided Comprehension in Questioning Text

I explain the process of leaving tracks to kids (see also Harvey and Goudvis 2000). I think it helps solidify the reason for which we are taking notes, that is, to be able to look back at them in order to *follow the trail* we have left. Just as Hansel and Gretel did!

I begin the process by explaining why it's important to leave tracks. I usually tell a bit of the story of Hansel and Gretel.

"They left stones and crumbs," I say, "but we have something better that we can use to help us remember. Sometimes, after I have read a chapter in preparation for my book club, I forget the things I want to talk about, so I put little sticky notes here and there as I read to remind me what I want to talk about and where it is in the chapter. I can follow them just like Hansel and Gretel followed the small white stones."

I then model that process for the group. I read a brief segment of text, stopping here and there to wonder aloud. I pick up a sticky, jot down my mnemonic (just a few words, or sometimes a picture or symbol) while saying it aloud, and then read on.

After I have demonstrated the technique, I pass five very small sticky notes to each student and remind the class to save a tree by turning the sticky note sideways to write, and then tearing off the unused part for the next entry (which should then have some sticky left on the end of it). Or, if their mnemonic takes up too much space, kids can also fold their notes over and use the back. Very small "ant writing" helps. If sticky notes are not available, teachers can cut up scrap paper

A fifth grader in Mikal Murray's class writes his response on a sticky when his teacher stops her read-aloud for a brief moment.

and pass out small piles to each student, which is far more amenable to students than filling up those big blank pages of a literature notebook.

ASSESSMENT: MONITORING COMPREHENSION ALONG A WRITTEN TRAIL

For two different purposes I like to occasionally collect the sticky notes. These tracks can become a written comprehension record for teachers, helping them peer inside a student's thinking in search of strengths, weaknesses, and direction for instruction. Sticky note collections can also unveil various response trail patterns. For example, several years ago when I was working with a group of third graders and collected their notes, I quickly realized that they all had obsessive-compulsive vocabulary behaviors. Practically every sticky note had a term on it that they wanted defined. Later, I discovered that their teacher had told them to put the words they didn't know on their stickies. Thus, that was *all* they did! Most patterns are not so extreme, but they still provide us with direction for instruction.

When I collect sticky notes for my own assessment purposes, I generally give the students an envelope into which they place their notes when they are finished with them, but I also remind them to number them in chronological order first. I then stick (or use glue for non-stickies) the notes onto sheets of blank copy paper, which makes filing and referencing easier (see Figure 4–1). Furthermore,

Figure 4–1 I collected this group of stickies from first grader Chrystal after the group had finished their *Amelia Bedelia* conversation.

Small-Group Response After Teacher Read-Alouds

follow-up student comprehension conferences allow me to jot notes directly onto their sticky note pages.

A student's self-generated thoughts on texts are often more revealing than the overused fill-in-someone-else's-blank workbook pages and blackline masters. Logged notes also become a first step in the necessary skill of notetaking and they lay a concrete trail for the comprehension strategy of referencing previous information for evidence—all of which needs to be modeled, modeled, modeled.

CONVERSATION TRIADS AFTER THE READ-ALOUD

Modeling a Triadic Interaction

So, what happens when the reading is over and everyone has sticky note reminders? I find it is helpful to first ask for a couple of volunteers to come forward and form a triad with me. However, sometimes this is not the best model if the teacher ends up doing most of the talking. So, after a brief interaction or two, I ask for another volunteer triad to come and sit in front of the rest of the group to demonstrate how their threesome might function—without the teacher.

Once the autonomous volunteer triad is sitting together and the rest of us are observing in fishbowl style, I like to first compliment the threesome on their structure. Then I suggest that one of them should just start by offering a wonder, to which I would expect the others to respond. I also remind them that the best conversations move back and forth and back and forth, staying on the same topic until it is "all used up." I do not criticize, but instead focus on all the positive elements of their sharing. It's not important that these precursor models be perfect. The class just needs the basic idea.

So, after a minute or two, when everyone is chomping at the bit to participate, I invite the others to move into their triads and begin their conversations. I also tell them that I will be floating from group to group, noting good things I hear and see happening. (See E in Figure 2–1 for this structure.) My observing and continual roaming seems to help keep groups focused.

Groups That Finish Early

At first, some triads will finish early. I solve this temporary problem in a variety of ways. When multiple copies of the book are not available, I copy pages from my read-aloud book to offer students in that finished group another chance to search for interesting items for conversation. Or sometimes I ask them to collaborate to develop a sketchy list of the topics that they covered during their conversation, after which they can search for other important topics that should be considered.

At other times, I ask them to use a rubric scale to evaluate their group's conversation and try to think of evidence that supports each score they log.

Above all, I *do not,* at this point, allow the group to move into a different activity. To do so is to validate their shallow response engagement. I am adamant about this because I now know full well that once students understand how conversations work, groups would stay together all day to discuss the book, if time allowed. Furthermore, if one triad is allowed to move into another activity, we all know that within two minutes, others would be following in their footsteps. In other words, kids come to understand that this is the period in which we get caught up in story talk and the conversation process. These early expectations are important. Above all: trust the kids.

Assessment: Teacher as a Roaming Observer

Throughout this triadic response period, the teacher, acting as a roaming observer, plays an important role. (See E of Figure 2–1.) When logging observations, I don't write anything negative, but try to find positive descriptors for every group as I quietly move from triad to triad. Obviously, students are motivated to perform when the teacher arrives at their side. Yet that performance will grow into natural response patterns once the students feel comfortable.

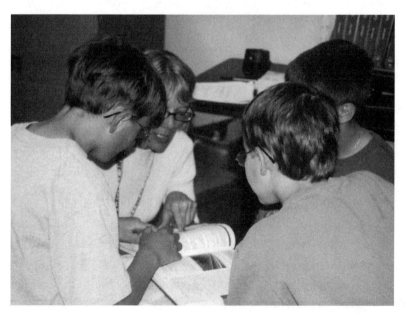

Teacher Barb McKay stops to support a triad that is investigating a reference.

It's important that the role of roaming observer is not confused with that of sergeant at arms. Slipping into the role of supervisor or manager encourages the kids to slip out of that role. It's the difference between whether we want to discipline the kids or whether we want them to discipline themselves. Most would opt for the latter. Thus, we focus on our role of observer, take copious positive notes, and afterward, celebrate all the good stuff we saw.

Sharing Positive Observations with Students

I allow only brief periods for those first autonomous conversations; therefore, after about ten minutes, I ask everyone to stop and return to the large-group setting. There, I share all my positive observations. This is always a proud and happy time, full of group smiles as I mention the variety of good things I saw. Following are some of the positive observations I might emphasize.

POSITIVE TEACHER OBSERVATIONS DURING CONVERSATIONS

- structures maintained ("This group stayed close together and worked cooperatively.")
- tentative responses ("I heard Ulin predict using *maybe, probably*, and *I bet*.")
- evidence to back thoughts and opinions ("I heard Marta say 'because' to introduce evidence for her ideas.")
- rich wonders ("I heard Joey say. . . .")
- rich conversations ("Deb's group really investigated the main character's actions. I heard. . . .")
- connections ("Juan's group connected this book to another one called. . . .")

This is also a time when I am able to add a few positive conversation behaviors that the group has not placed on the room's chart yet. Thus, if time allows, the last question I ask is: "Can anyone think of anything else we should add to our class' conversation chart?"

ANALYTICAL, CRITICAL, AND EVALUATIVE RESPONSES: GUIDED COMPREHENSION IN MAKING CONNECTIONS

In their book on comprehension strategies, Harvey and Goudvis (2000) tell us that making connections to text is one of the key factors related to comprehension. That is, the more we connect, the more we understand and remember; so if students have prior knowledge related to their reading, they will then connect and build on that knowledge, those experiences. Without such foundational connections, students cannot extrapolate, synthesize, deduce, and infer. Even regurgitating facts becomes difficult when those facts are connected to nothing. Connecting is a key element in comprehending.

However, not only will such connections enhance comprehension, they will also enrich conversations and draw kids into higher levels of thinking. The Connections Venn (Figure 4–2) is a handy visual that invites students into several kinds of connections. It provides them with a concrete mental framework that can be accessed during reading, throughout conversations, while answering assessment questions, and also during response writing, and it scaffolds them toward making associations that enrich their reading, writing, comprehension, and conversations.

The Connections Venn

The Connections Venn consists of two levels: (1) the base (bottom) level, that is, the genre scheme inside the text itself, and (2) the secondary (top) level, which incorporates elements inside the reader that relate to those inside the text. At the base level, over which the Venn is laid, there exist the fundamental elements of the narrative. Such elements remain the substance of the story, as well as the conversation. They include the characters, setting, problem, events, plot, theme, and resolution. Because topics and comprehension grow out of these narrative elements, literature conversations should stay connected to them.

Yet conversations are also peppered with the thoughts, ideas, passions, and experiences of the reader, all of which become the key ingredients within the three overlapping circles that make up the Venn. The fewer connections the reader can make to the story elements, the less she will comprehend. Therefore, the final product should be a story-grounded and reader-connected conversation.

Students come to understand that they can connect in myriad ways to aspects of the text. Most commonly, they associate their own lives, family members, friends, or worldly experiences with the characters, events, and setting in the text.

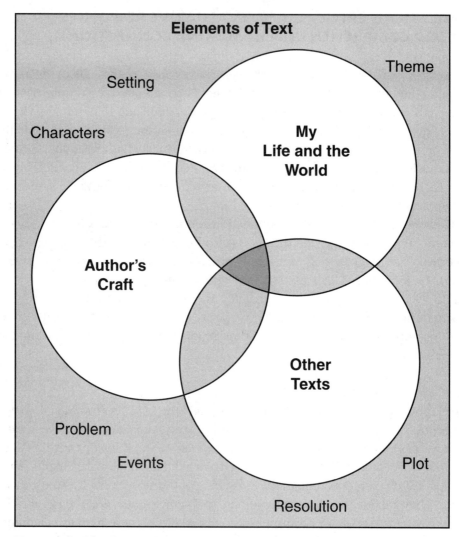

Figure 4–2   The Connections Venn

Therefore, one piece of the Connections Venn focuses on the category "My Life and the World." At other times, the text will remind the reader of something she has read, heard, or viewed, that is, a book, an article, a movie, or some other text. This aspect of the Venn is simply labeled "Other Texts." The final type of connection readers make is to the writing of that particular author. They notice the use of dialogue, metaphor, illustrations, characterization, and a raft of other traits that fall under the "Author's Craft" heading.

Children are never too young to start making these connections. A two-year-old will connect the doggy in the picture to his own doggy, calling that illustrated canine by his own dog's name. A five-year-old will relate feelings or experiences he has had to those of a character. A very small child will question discrepancies between a book and its movie. Even aspects of an author's craft are noticed by the very young. For example, many three-year-olds are able to point out Dr. Suess books by the author's style, illustrations, and humor. All of these children are—through their own experiences—making connections to story. All of them are delving into rich and rewarding ways to talk about books. It is from all of this that comprehension gathers its form. The Connections Venn will support this. Let's see how it can be a handy, concrete guide for making connections.

Kinds of Connections

Connections to My Life and the World

Everything we read, view, and hear evokes a life or world connection, making these more personal associations by far the most common. Harvey and Goudvis (2000) call these "text-to-self" and "text-to-world" connections. I combine their two categories because it is often difficult to discern one's self from one's world. Regardless, such connections are developed frequently in all conversations. For instance, a student who had just read *Tales of a Fourth Grade Nothing*, a story about a family with one particularly testy little boy, commented, "Peter reminds me of my little brother. He sure gets into trouble!" This student is connecting a facet of his own life—his brother—to a character in the text.

Students in my multiage, 1–2 classroom made this kind of connection during their conversation related to *My Father's Dragon*. Watch how Jen's connections to the real world evoke a fact versus fiction response from her peers.

Jen: I was wondering, you know, you know how on a real globe, I don't think there's such a thing called New Island, Wild Island.

Amy: There might be. [*lengthy silence then* . . .]

Amy: [*again*] But, it's a make-up story.

Fallon: Yeah, it's a made-up story.

When a group of Amy Patterson's second graders were discussing Roald Dahl's *Matilda*, their text-to-world connections made for rich conversation grist.

This group of girls is trying to figure out why the characters in the book call the TV a "tellie," and again, the fact/fiction question arises.

Tiana:　I wonder why they call the TV "the tellie."

Anna:　[laughing] Yeah, really!

Ellie:　Probably because they watch TV so much.

Jennie:　Or maybe they watch the show that's called *The TV Tellie*.

Ellie:　Or maybe they watch *Teletubbies* or something.

Jennie:　I don't think they had *Teletubbies* back then.

Tiana:　It wouldn't be back then, because it's not a true story.

Girls:　Oh, yeah—

Tiana:　They didn't have *Teletubbies* back then. Or, maybe they did?

Just as common as world connections are self connections. During a conversation rooted in *Roll of Thunder, Hear My Cry*, a child in Kirsten Baetzhold's third grade disagreed with another student's calculations of a character's age. Debating the issue, Lasandra made the following text-to-self connection: "Yeah, but they're still kids. Our age! They're not twenty! They're *our* age!"

A fifth grader discussing *The Great Gilly Hopkins* mades the following text-to-self connection: "She's looking for somebody who loves her, but I would hate it if my mother didn't love me, if she abandoned me [which is what Gilly's mother did]. I mean, she had to find out [that her mother had abandoned her]."

Even very young children can readily connect text to their own realms. This then becomes a natural entre into the study of character traits, personalities, motives, feelings, and such. Dredging out these elements in a text helps students not only to understand the characters but also to better understand themselves and those in their own world. It is a natural seedbed for compassion, empathy, and understanding, which unfolds again and again during conversations at every grade level. Indeed, the aforementioned groups discussed the misfortune of Gilly, the injustices cast upon the blacks, and the intelligence of Matilda.

Even preschoolers make such connections between their worlds, themselves, and the texts they are experiencing! Most of us have seen a toddler point to the picture of a woman and say, "Mommy." Such connections broaden their world and help them categorize and recatagorize its elements.

Some of these preschoolers are trying to figure out the codes of language, which can be seen in their connections related to the system of symbols that we use. For instance, when three-year-old Delanie was listening to her grandmother read a story's title and the author's name, the preschooler pointed to the letters and asked, "Does that spell my birthday?" Delanie had just experienced a birthday with her name spelled across the cake. She, just as others, was making a connection between the unknown (the sign system of language) and the known (her name on her birthday cake). Such world and self connections permeate our lives from birth onward. As a matter of fact, it is how we learn.

Connections to the author's craft

Readers can also make connections to the author's craft, that is, the author's style, his use of dialogue, illustration support, book length, sentence length, vocabulary load—in other words, the same kinds of connections we, as adults, make to the craft of the authors we read. We readers often speak vehemently regarding an author's craft. We say, "She did not develop her characters enough!" or "Her use of dialogue is what made that book!" or "The book would have been much better had it been half its length," or "I'm not reading that! His sentences are sixty words long!"

At first, kids' connections to the author's craft are minimal. However, when we teachers model craft connections, and when students are encouraged to compare and contrast one author's works or the works of different authors, such comparisons will eventually work their way into conversations. Furthermore, students who are heavily involved in the writing process will begin early to notice the craft of others. They will talk about it and emulate it. Teachers who point out the use of dialogue, metaphor, alliteration, and other language elements will have students who begin to notice these in the work of the authors they are reading—even in kindergarten and first grade!

The following list provides some author's craft connections that can be modeled for students:

AUTHOR'S CRAFT CONNECTIONS

- patterns of rhyme, rhythm, and repetition
- font size, spacing, and placement
- illustrations that support or extend

Small-Group Response After Teacher Read-Alouds

What did you notice?

My first graders used to readily make author's craft connections, even at the beginning of the year. Part of the motivation came from me continually asking: "What did you notice this time?" One year in October I was introducing *The Jigaree*, a Joy Cowley book, to the class. I had just finished modeling it for the kids when John gestured an "Aha!" We asked him what he had noticed and he replied that *The Jigaree* was "just like that other book we read."

"Which book?" I asked.

John jumped up, excitedly ran over to our library corner, and after a very brief search, came back with a book called *Happy or Sad*. He opened it and compared several pages, showing us the repetitious pattern the author had used. John then drew our attention back to *The Jigaree* and its repetitious pattern. Indeed, both authors used repetition in their craft. As a matter of fact, Joy Cowley is probably the queen of patterned texts for kids.

If early primary-age students make author's craft connections, it is obvious that older students can also. When kids are invited to notice something, they do! Let's investigate some of their observations related to the author's craft.

Let's look again at those fourth graders who were discussing *Toliver's Travels* and hypothesizing who the character Dicey might be. One member of the group suggested that Dicey may be an orphan. Examining an illustration, another member commented, "She just looks—she fits the description and her hair and all, I think she's having a hard time in her life." Notice how this student ties the author's description to the illustration, both parts of craft.

A small group of students in my multiage 1–2 class were just beginning *My Father's Dragon*. The title baffled them so much that one question after another related to the seeming mismatch between title and text. Notice how these students are investigating the particular traits of this author.

> *Jen:* You know, when I'm looking at this title, you know how sometimes the cover gives you an idea of what the book is about?

Fallon:	Yeah.
Jen:	Well, not with this book!
Fallon:	I would think that if it's called *My Father's Dragon* that, like, the first chapter it would say, like, about where he's going and that he's going to meet a dragon.
Jen:	Yeah, even in *Charlotte's Web*, I mean, it tells about Charlotte *before* he met her.

It is easy to see the overlap here between the author's craft and other texts when Jen contrasts the seeming mismatch in *My Father's Dragon* to the meaningful title-text match of E. B. White's book. It is also easy to see the ways in which multiple and overlapping connections enrich a conversation.

Using biography to enhance connections to author's craft

We are so fortunate, because today's literary world offers kids biographies on many well-known authors. These come in many shapes and sizes, from books to audios to videos, from easy picture books to difficult pictureless texts. Using a biography in its entirety will underlay that author's work with a foundation for connections. Strategically using just a portion of a biography can also be useful in that it helps to target instruction in a specific area. For instance, playing a section of the Dr. Suess video biography *In Search of Dr. Suess* helps readers make connections to certain facets of his writing, for example, his bent on political activism in the form of satire.

I could list numerous biographical resources; however, I cannot come close to what the Internet can afford through a common search engine. Therefore, that is exactly what I suggest using.

Connections to other texts

Let's look at that third connection, other texts. Here, the term *text* holds a far wider connotation than just books. It can mean spoken, written, aural, or viewed text; therefore, it includes radio, television, dictionaries, newspapers, brochures, interviews, speeches, movies, and many other forms of communication. Students enjoy making a list of everything a text can be, and they seem to like the fact that it is acceptable to compare and contrast their present text with movies, television, and other out-of-school books.

A strong connection to other texts arose when a whole-class circle was discussing *My Side of the Mountain*. Mikal Murrays's fifth graders were struggling to understand the time frame of the book within the context of foreshadowing, a concept that can confuse even adult readers. The students had little background or literary language in foreshadowing, but using other similar texts, they worked together, attempting to figure it out.

Andy: I think it was talking about *before* the snowstorm.

Agatha: Isn't he talking about the snowstorm? "I am holed up in a snowstorm." And then, he gets into when it comes up, and now it's probably gonna end.

Allie: And then, the second chapter is called "I Get Started on This Venture," so then it starts telling the story about—

Nadine: You know how in movies, like when it starts out?

Said: Yeah, like *Titanic*.

Nadine: Yeah, and in *Evita*, it starts out as her funeral, but then it shows her as a little girl.

Sean: It does?!

Nadine: [*at the same time as Joey*] It shows her when she was really old!

Joey: Yeah, it does. Yeah, it shows Rose when she's really old, and then it starts telling about the story, and then, like, pieces of Rose comes back and tells more. And then it goes back to the movie and then Rose talks and then it goes back to the movie.

As these fifth graders struggled to make meaning, it helped them to compare a literary technique in their book with a similar one used in movies they'd seen. The connection settled their minds and carved a foundational experience for what they would someday come to know as a facet of an author's craft called foreshadowing. At this point, however, they were collecting pieces of meaning from several texts whose authors had used that particular device. What a perfect time for a related minilesson!

A group of second graders was also helped to make meaning by comparing the text they were reading, *Matilda*, to another whose main character they decided had similar traits. Here, they attempt to understand Matilda's genius through another text that also had a genius in it.

Jennie: I know, but she [Matilda] has a calculator in her mind that has all the facts for her.

Girls: Uh-huh. Yeah.

Jennie:	So she knows it right away, so when she asks her a question, she's like [*snaps her fingers to show immediacy*], it's in her mind.
Ellie:	It's not like a pocket calculator—
Jennie:	It's like a *brain* calculator!
Ellie:	It's like, like [*spins her finger at the side of the head to demonstrate thinking*], Cam Jansen! Remember her?
Jennie:	Yeah. It's like her—uh—like her—uh—
Tiana:	Yeah, it's like a photographic memory, you know.
Jennie:	Actually like a math book that tells you all the answers.
Ellie:	Yeah, Cam's is like a math book. That's like the same thing [*snaps her fingers again*]. She remembers it right away.

These girls came to understand more about the character traits of Matilda through another character they all knew, Cam Jansen. They connected to a character in another text, while at the same time focusing on their book's character. They could just as well have connected events to events, setting to setting, or any of the other common story elements. Through these connections, each new text finds its place within an entire network of meanings, each supporting, complementing, and extending its forerunners. There can be no doubt that students' comprehension is enhanced through the teaching of these connection strategies.

Introducing the Connections Venn
Coloring the Venn circles
The first time I share the Connections Venn with students, I give them each a copy, and then we talk about one element at a time, after which they color one circle red, another blue, and the final one yellow. I find it helps kids remember Venn attributes when we add color to the picture.

We begin by using a common text—either something they've all been listening to, a text they've been reading, or a popular movie they've all seen. I link that common text to my own self and world, and then invite the class to make some of their own connections. We start with self and world connections because they are the easiest.

What does this remind you of?
I always begin the connections process by asking, "What does this remind you of?" For instance, if we had just read *The Grasshopper and the Ants*, I might ask,

"Do those ants remind you of anyone you know? They remind me of my friend because she is such a hard worker and always ends up sharing with others."

I draw the students' attention to the way in which I usually give evidence for my connection; that is, I don't just tell *what* it reminds me of, but I also tell *why* it reminds me of that specific thing, person, or event. And I draw their attention to the fact that I frequently use the word *because* in my explanation, at which point a quick reference to our own Statement-Evidence anchor chart connects new learning to old.

Guiding students toward explaining connections

After my example, the kids freely make similar connections within their own lives and world. This is the period in which I continually draw them out, asking them for explanations for their connections. My probing example encourages the students themselves to follow a classmate's brief connection with, "Why does it remind you of that?" And we use the Statement-Evidence chart to log our connections. Or, you may want to scribe their connections on a separate chart, using this new example as an anchor experience.

Later, I model in the same way how we can connect to the contents in the other two Venn circles, but I always draw attention to the fact that any connection can cross over into more than one Venn area; that is why the circles overlap. I explain this over and over again through a variety of examples, continually reminding students of these connections throughout read-alouds on following days. Each read-aloud presents the perfect forum for reinforcement and review, so I implement it almost every time we crack open a book.

Taking the Venn to the Conversation Floor

Not long after this introduction I invite students to move the concept into their own conversation realm. That is, one day, after they finish their conversations, I ask the kids to think back on their discussions and decide how they connected what was said in their conversations to the Venn areas.

We meet in a class group to discuss these connections. When students contribute a connection, we ask them to explain its relationship to the text. For example, Clyde, a kindergartner, made a connection to his own life, and we guided his comprehension by asking him to explain that connection. He told us, "Timmy had a dog just like my dog," so we asked, "How is your dog like Timmy's?"

Clyde responded, "My dog doesn't listen as well as his. Mine gets into trouble *all* the time." This young reader is using his own life here to both compare and contrast with that of a text character. Thus, Clyde was guided toward a higher level of response, connection, and ultimately comprehension.

Jennifer offered, "I made a connection using other texts." When asked to explain, she responded, "The other day when I was looking through my mom's magazine, I noticed an article about Alaska. It showed all these neat places. And it told about dog sledding. It even showed what they look like. So, when you were reading about that in the story, I had that picture in my mind because of the magazine. I told the kids in my group about the picture in the magazine."

Occasionally bringing small-group connections back into a large-group share demonstrates the variety of ways in which connections can be made. Furthermore, it validates numerous perspectives related to the same topic or idea and moves kids into higher levels of reasoning and comprehension. I want my students to understand that rarely is there one right answer to higher-level questions.

ASSESSMENT: A LITERATURE CONVERSATION GROUP PROCESSING RUBRIC

Heidi Clarke and her class developed a group checklist similar to the individual checklist used in Chapter 2 to be used when students had completed a day's conversation experience. Note that students need to come to consensus on each item listed. This sometimes provokes disagreements that need to be resolved before group members can sign off on their quarter-page assessment sheet. Once all have signed it, it is assumed that all have agreed. It's easy to see how coming to consensus on these items would scaffold students toward the metacognition needed in mature conversation assessment.

Literature Conversation Group Processing Rubric
by Heidi Clarke and Class

_____ Did we sit together in a group, knee to knee, eye to eye?
_____ Was everyone prepared?
_____ Did we stay on the topic?
_____ Did we respond to everyone's wonders?
_____ Did we invite everyone in?
_____ Did we piggyback onto another's response?
_____ Did we look back in the book?
_____ Did we make connections to the plot?
_____ Characters? _____ Setting? _____ Events?

_____ Did we make connections to our own lives and the world?
_____ Did we make connections to other texts?
_____ Did we make connections to the author's craft?

All members of your group should sign below if you agree on the above answers.

_____   _____
_____   _____
_____   _____

Date:

CHARTING CONNECTION TYPES: RESPONSE TRAILS

There's another tool we can use to scaffold this connections process into a comprehensible skill. I construct a three-column chart with one Venn area heading each column. As students give a variety of connections, I jot each down in the appropriate column. Then, the kids like to come up and sign their initials beside each of their contributions. We save this chart for its reference anchors.

For example, here is the way I would chart some of the preceding connections:

Text Connections We Have Made		
My Life and World	_Author's Craft_	_Other Texts_
Clyde's dog/ Tim's dog	Repetition	Magazine pic. of Alaskan sled
New Island/ not real	Description	_Titanic/Evita/My Side of Mt._
TV/tellie	Titles match text	_Matilda/Cam_
Gillie's mom/ my mom	Foreshadowing	_Jansen_

Making connections is the way in which we learn. Connections are keys to comprehension. Therefore, the Connections Venn can play a very important part in making reading and conversations more meaningful. Children come to understand that good readers always tie their outside world to the inside world of text. The Venn just helps to make the experience a bit more concrete—so concrete that it even works with primary students!

ASSESSMENT: CHARTING CONNECTIONS TO TEXT

Students will make far more connections if they are encouraged to assess their conversations for connections. One easy way to do this is to ask groups to use the same kind of three-column chart that was demonstrated in the previous section after they finish a conversation. Later, invite the entire class together to share group connections.

Another way to do this is to have students come forward and place their connections stickies in the appropriate column on a large class connections chart. That is, if a student's note stated, "Reminds me of *Where the Wild Things Are*. Scary!" he would paste his sticky note in the column labeled "Connections to Other Texts."

When we did this in Heidi Clarke's fourth grade, we quickly came to realize that most of our wonders fell in primarily one area. Once the students realized this, they tried to stretch themselves during their following conversations. We even heard kids say, "We haven't mentioned anything about the author's craft."

As a matter of routine, the second graders in Sheila Delmonte's class would review each Venn area during their postconversation assessment. It's not surprising that, knowing they would be assessing for those traits, the kids tried more diligently to incorporate them into conversations. In this way, assessment drove the process.

*A fifth grader in Mikal Murray's class,
intensely engaged in making her point*

CLASSROOMS IN ACTION:
STUDENT SMALL-GROUP RESPONSE TO TEACHER READ-ALOUDS

The students in Mr. Fen's class were becoming very excited about literature conversations. Just yesterday they had observed and discussed the large-circle conversation that their teacher had videotaped by setting the camera on a tripod that was focused on the group. Pleased with their progress, everyone agreed it was time to move on to the next step in the process.

As Mr. Fen picked up the book he would be using for the read-aloud, Heather asked, "Are we going to videotape again today, Mr. Fen?" Immediately, most of the students stopped what they were doing to hear their teacher's response.

"No," responded the teacher. "We're going to be doing something a little different. I think you will like this even more than the large-group conversations we've been having. You'll have a greater opportunity to share your own thoughts, because we'll be meeting in much smaller groups called triads or quads."

At this point Mr. Fen described the new structure and then informed class members in which group each would participate. "But before you move into your small groups, you'll need to join me on the rug with your pencil and clipboard. First, I'll be reading to you," announced the teacher. So the students gathered their things and joined their teacher on the rug.

Before Mr. Fen began reading, he called one triad forward to demonstrate the structure of their postreading groups. Then he opened the book to begin his demonstration of notetaking with sticky notes. He had planned to use his read-aloud period that week to entice the class to learn more about the fantasy genre by reading a chapter from a different piece of fantasy each day. Mr. Fen knew from past experience that it would whet their appetites for that genre. *Harry Potter and the Sorcerer's Stone* was that day's selection.

After a brief explanation of why he was carrying a small stack of stickies, the teacher quickly introduced the book and then began reading to his eager listeners. But before he finished the second page, he stopped and said, "I wonder what it meant when it said he 'noticed the first sign of something peculiar'? I'm going to write 'peculiar sign' on a sticky note and stick it right down at the bottom of this page in the book. I'll leave a little jutting out so I can easily retrieve it." He then tore off the unused part of the sticky note, saving it for later, and went on to the next page.

About halfway down the second page, the teacher stopped and wondered aloud, "What's going on here? People in cloaks. Cats reading. Weird! I am going to write 'cloaks? cats?' on this note because I would like to talk in my group about what those might mean. If you want to talk about those in your triad, you can also put them on one of your sticky notes." He waited for a few seconds for those who chose to write. And then he went on.

After Mr. Fen had read some of the next page, he stopped once more and asked, "I wonder why this guy dislikes the Potters so much?" He took another sticky and announced, "I am going to write 'dislikes Potters' with a question mark after it on this one."

94

Then the teacher invited the group to write anything they were wondering about on their own sticky notes. He also reminded the kids that they should use as few words as possible, just enough to jog their memories when they glanced at their notes later on.

After a minute or two, he went on reading several more paragraphs before again stopping to invite the students to write wonders. This continued through a couple more pages until Mr. Fen interrupted to say, "I have just introduced you to a piece of fiction from the fantasy genre. I'll put it on the shelf, in case anyone wants to continue reading it during SSR. Tomorrow I'll read another example of this genre, a book by Roald Dahl. Each day this week I'll introduce you to another fantasy book, after which it will be shelved so you can read it, if you like. Now, let's move into conversation triads, remembering everything we've learned to make our conversations work well."

The students were excited to meet with their friends, but some groups had quite a time deciding where they would sit. Finally, after everyone seemed to be knee to knee in tight triads and quads, Mr. Fen grabbed his clipboard and canvassed the room. He stopped here and there to jot a note of praise, which he would later be pleased to share.

After what seemed to be only a brief length of time, Mr. Fen noticed that a group on the other side of the room appeared to be finished. He walked over to them and asked how things were going, to which they responded, "We're done!"

"Well, then," responded the teacher, "think about the rubric we did. Then the three of you should decide whether your conversation deserves a 1, 2, or 3. Afterward, Brad, I'd like you to scribe for the group as each member gives reasons to verify the score he or she chose. You can also use the conversation chart to help." Mr. Fen then left the group, knowing they would have to struggle to prove they deserved a 3. But he also knew that it was far better that they—rather than he—do the judging.

The teacher stopped the other groups after about ten minutes, knowing it was better to stop them while they were still involved and interested. Students were pleased to hear all the good things their teacher had logged while observing their triads. Afterward, Mr. Fen asked, "Does anyone have anything else we should add to our conversation chart?"

"I know one," responded Marilyn. "Be patient."

"Good one," complimented the teacher. "And we all learned how to do that when we were in the big circle, didn't we?" He then invited Marilyn to add her thought to the chart. When no one else offered a new idea, Mr. Fen shelved *Harry Potter* and invited the group to prepare for lunch. Before leaving for lunch, however, he noticed that someone had already borrowed *Harry Potter*.

FINISHING TOUCHES

If a camcorder is available, it can add a grand incentive. So, after the class' first experience in independent triads, I suggest to them that when they become a little more experienced, I will bring in the camcorder and record some of their conversations. Tape recorders can also be used, but audiotapes will not provide nearly as much information as a video does. Watching themselves on tape allows students to observe their own conversations for positive traits, and it is the most motivating factor in leading the group to optimal performance.

I try to invite the literature conversation triads into several of these experiences throughout the week, and after they are comfortable and functioning well, I do videotape them. They love seeing themselves on television and can always find a raft of positive elements. Very giddy at first, they soon mature beyond stardom and seriously consider what they are observing. Only after this step seems secure do I move on to Step 5, in which triadic conversations are grounded in the students' independent reading of text.

Chapter 5

AUTONOMOUS RESPONSE TRIADS AFTER INDEPENDENT READING

Collecting reviews of the volume under discussion not only provides a number of perspectives, but also shows the peccadilloes and prejudices of the reviewers in a particularly clear light— good training for book group discussion.

Sandra and Spayde, The Joy of Conversation (2001, 157)

Step by step, chapter by chapter we've walked together down this book's conversation pathways, and with each new leg of the journey our students have acquired greater independency. As a consequence, in this final portion the teacher is no longer reading the book for the students, nor is she actively participating in their small-group conversations. Instead, our book groups can now emulate adult book clubs, where, after reading a common text independently, participants respond to that text and to each other in competent little talk groups, "where the imagination is free to explore."

AUTONOMY IN READING AND DISCUSSION AT LAST!

This means that during this part of the process, teachers do not read the text or a section of the text before small groups discuss it. Instead, kids read the material themselves, jotting mnemonic notes here and there for reference when their group meets. After reading, students move into triads (or quads) for conversation, just as they did in the last step.

Optimally, groups should now be able to carry on a literature conversation without the teacher's continuous presence and input. This means that while one group is participating in a literature conversation, the teacher is free to work with other students. She might present a minilesson in another area of the room or she might confer with individual students to assess or scaffold them in their reading and writing. However, during some of these independent conversations I like to serve as their silent observer, collecting positive tidbits that can later be shared.

Depending on the story, the group, the group members, or the time of day, I might touch base with the conversation cohort frequently or seldom. That is, if the students have already had a reading instructional period and their conversations follow sustained silent reading (SSR), then I usually allow them far more autonomy. However, if they are discussing the text after a guided or shared reading experience, I join the group more often. Just another of the ongoing decisions we, as professionals, must make!

WHAT ABOUT PARTNERING AND CALLING THE CIRCLE?

Just because students are now capable of conversation autonomy does not mean that we look at partnering and calling the circle as events of the past. Certainly not. They continue to serve us well during class read-alouds in all subject areas. Almost every time I read aloud I model a strategy or skill and then invite students to partner, because the more experience they have, the more skilled they become. But just as important, by stopping for partners to share, I am more assured of the group's attention throughout, because they know they will have opportunities to exercise their own voices. Thus, partnering remains an important part of almost every day.

Furthermore, there is always something new to model, to scaffold. Every book, every genre has its own particular properties that can be illuminated through demonstration. It is those that I model and invite students to respond to through a partnering protocol. After such modeling, I like to invite the group into participation and observe their responses; it is then that I call the circle.

CONVERSATIONS AFTER SUSTAINED SILENT READING

Some teachers like to invite students into response triads after SSR. That is, they create a classroom context whereby triads can select from available multiple copies of texts. Each day, students preplan—with or without the teacher—the amount their group will read to prepare for the next conversation. Some of the slower readers take their books home to get a head start. Then, after SSR they move into their triads.

I used this method in my multiage classroom and it worked quite well, especially when triads ordered their multiple copies from our monthly book orders. However, before I realized it, such groups, while planning for their reading, would implore that I scour the school in search of one more copy of this book or that. But it was worth it overall, because the students were so dedicated to the reading and the conversation process.

Using SSR as the outlet for narrative texts seems to work well in the intermediate grades, because by then, many teachers have moved into content area texts for their guided reading instructional period. Usually, by third grade, most students have had three years of daily guided reading using narratives. Why not turn the tables in the intermediate grades? That is, save the narratives for SSR followed by literature conversations.

CONVERSATIONS AFTER GUIDED READING

Guided reading is used during what we normally consider the reading period, a time when the teacher scaffolds students through instructional-level texts. It is a time for teaching, for skill instruction, for strategy instruction. Therefore, I do not often invite postreading conversations into the structure of a guided reading group. The reason is obvious; there is just not enough time for everything.

Yet there will always be some occasions for conversations, even when using guided reading. For instance:

- ◆ during exceptionally exciting parts of the book or story
- ◆ after a few days of guided oral reading and teacher direction
- ◆ when the text is easier than expected

Preparing for a postreading conversation during SSR

♦ when an interesting issue presents itself and students need time to debate and discuss before going on

To be sure, I would not recommend inviting conversations *after* the group hashes over the story with the teacher. Kids should always enter their conversations with unrehearsed interactions. Otherwise, stories lose their richness.

CONVERSATIONS FOR STUDENTS WHO CANNOT DECODE TEXT

Reading ability should not be the gatekeeper for conversation participation. Delanie could ask questions about text at age three! Students unable to decode text are still able to "read" wordless books—that is, well-conceived picture books—in order to share their thoughts and connections. Young children will readily return to pictures to explain and provide evidence to back their thinking.

Teachers of non- or novice readers who are using a reading series can give each child a copy of the book. If the story is rich, all the teacher will have to do to prepare the students is create a backdrop and then invite the kids to read the pictures, place a sticky note here or there, jot a reminder on it, and be ready to share when the group meets.

However, some reading series contain shallow pieces that have little or no actual story value. Even some of the popular patterned texts tend to possess little story value. It might be best to avoid these for conversations, and instead, select other, richer story texts. Obviously, multiple copies will need to be available so that each group has a common text. For books with words, it usually works better to do a shared reading for novices before they do their own reading. Be aware, though, that conversations will be shallow if discussion takes place *during* the shared reading, because it is almost guaranteed that the teacher's voice will predominate and generally the same kids will always respond.

Regardless, all students should sometimes have the opportunity to be completely independent. Most important: trust the kids.

BUT HOW WILL I KNOW WHAT THEY'RE DOING?

Teachers barely begin implementing the independent triads before an accountability question arises: How will I know what is happening in a conversation group if *I* am not there? For many teachers, this is a very intimidating situation. They worry about losing control. They worry about what might be discussed with no teacher present. And, they worry about how they can evaluate students, when they

Preparing for conversation with a sticky note

themselves are not participating in the conversation. However, there are numerous ways to ameliorate those worries.

First of all, it is unnecessary that the teacher know every single transaction that takes place in the room. Students can learn even when the teacher is *not* present. However, it does make sense to monitor these conversation triads to some extent. That can be accomplished through a variety of avenues. For instance, the teacher can videotape independent groups, invite groups to assess their conversations afterward, ask a few students to serve as roaming observers who jot observation notes, or ask students to complete a written response as a sequel to their conversation.

Mikal Murray sometimes asks her fifth graders to write her a letter (see Figure 5–1) about what they have read and the connections they've made. She keeps these in their literacy portfolios to track progress in written response. They become predictors for the more formal assessments that they will have to take. Mikal also responds to each student's writing, attempting to scaffold each forward in his or her growth.

ASSESSMENT: USING A CAMCORDER

Getting Started

Classroom videotaping may seem to be an intimidating process for the inexperienced. Anyone unsure of this kind of technology should try seeking the aid of another teacher who may have a planning period free to tape. Teachers are the most generous people in the world and are usually happy to assist a colleague who is getting started on a new adventure. Besides, the process may become contagious!

In today's technological world, many teachers have camcorders in their homes, even if the school does not own one. I used our family's equipment at first, and then received a grant for a camcorder for the classroom—twice!

The camcorder can be mounted on a tripod that is focused on the conversation group throughout their dialogue. The teacher does not even have to be present! Some of my own students' conversations (whose transcripts you've read) were captured in this manner. And, they were better without me standing over them!

Videotaping is very effective. Students want to look their best, and they usually try hard to do just that. Some students overtry and the footage ends up sounding like a performance, which, to some extent, no doubt it is. Yet camcorders will still serve to oversee what is happening in the group when the teacher, herself,

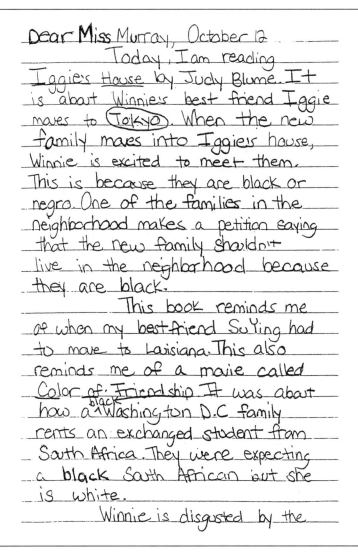

Dear Miss Murray,   October 12
         Today, I am reading
Iggie's House by Judy Blume. It
is about Winnie's best friend Iggie
moves to (Tokyo). When the new
family moves into Iggie's house,
Winnie is excited to meet them.
This is because they are black or
negro. One of the families in the
neighborhood makes a petition saying
that the new family shouldn't
live in the neighborhood because
they are black.
         This book reminds me
of when my best friend Su Ying had
to move to Louisiana. This also
reminds me of a movie called
Color of Friendship. It was about
how a black Washington D.C family
rents an exchanged student from
South Africa. They were expecting
a black South African but she
is white.
         Winnie is disgusted by the

Figure 5–1   A student's postconversation follow-up letter to Mikal Murray, the teacher

(Continued)

Autonomous Response Triads After Independent Reading

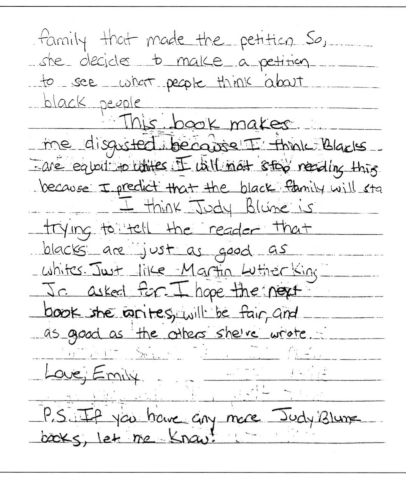

family that made the petition. So,
she decides to make a petition
to see what people think about
black people

This book makes
me disgusted because I think Blacks
are equal to whites. I will not stop reading this
because I predict that the black family will sta
I think Judy Blume is
trying to tell the reader that
blacks are just as good as
whites. Just like Martin Luther King
Jr. asked for. I hope the next
book she writes, will be fair, and
as good as the others she've wrote.

Love, Emily

P.S. If you have any more Judy Blume
books, let me know!

Figure 5–1 *continued*

cannot be present. Furthermore, the more often students have such an experience, the more natural they become in front of a camera.

Multiple Uses of Videotapes
These in-process videos can also be a wonderful tool during parent conferences. That is, in many cases, pictures can be worth a thousand words. Parents appreciate the privilege of viewing their child in a literate act, so I use them every year for that purpose.

A follow-up aspect related to videotaping that usually must be addressed is the sharing of what is taped with the students themselves. Kids can't wait to see themselves and their group on the screen. But this can be somewhat time-consuming—mostly because the kids giggle throughout the first showing. (Adults do this, too!) Therefore, in order to have them seriously investigate the tape for its positive aspects, they usually need to view it a second time.

To solve part of the time-consumption problem, I recommend that the teacher invite the group to a first viewing in some isolated corner, where no one other than those who participated can view the tape. They can be invited to respond to the tape (as a group or individually) by writing a critique related to what they found especially positive. Or, they can be asked to log the VCR's tracking numbers corresponding to the best portions of the tape. In that way, if the teacher prefers, she can fast-forward to the designated parts during a second viewing. Yet that does not preclude showing the whole conversation, if time allows.

The bottom line here again is that the students are constantly evaluating what makes conversations work well and sharing this with each other and their teacher. Even my first graders could do this!

Leigh-Ann Hildreth pauses the VCR as her first graders take a moment to examine their videotaped conversation.

ASSESSMENT: USING A CHECKLIST

Checklists are one of the easiest ways to assess a conversation. Groups can even develop one of their own (inspired by the conversation chart they've been constructing throughout each of the preceding steps), and it can be reproduced and used again and again. Asking students to discuss each point and then mark the ones that reflect the group's interactions can be very effective, because students do tend to be quite honest. Such checklists can be either individual or group assessments, shared together or simply handed in for teacher appraisal.

ASSESSMENT: USING A RUBRIC SCALE

Another effective form of assessment makes use of a rubric scale. Implementing rubric-driven assessments after literature conversations evokes in-depth discussion that focuses on the nuts and bolts of the event. Collaboratively developed rubrics work best because the kids know them inside out. The first step is deciding what the general categories or domains will be.

Categorizing Elements for Rubric Domains

This initial step attempts to categorize all conversation behaviors and content under several common domains. To develop a foundation for this process, teachers can reference state standards documents at *<www.statestandards.com>*. Be aware that many states do not include an oral language component in their English language arts standards. Nevertheless, some of those that do provide a great starting point.

New York's state standards documents can be one of these resources, particularly the document that describes pieces to be included in an elementary-level portfolio, which New York State calls the *Primary Literacy Profiles* (1999). In this document a rubric is provided through which teachers can assess classroom oral language behaviors, that is, listening and speaking. The *Primary Literacy Profiles* include four domains: (1) responsiveness, (2) participation, (3) clarity, and (4) organization. I have used these four categories, along with one more—content—successfully many times.

The International Reading Association (IRA) and the National Council of Teachers of English (NCTE) have also developed categories for "how students should be able to use language": (1) clearly, (2) strategically, (3) critically, and (4) creatively. Each of these is described in length on pages 20 and 21 of their *Standards for the English Language Arts* (1996), where content and behavior descriptors are included under each of the four categories. These could help with the organization and categorization of conversation chart elements. Another website, *<www.marcopolo.org>*, collaborates with several professional organizations to develop supportive information.

However, teachers do not have to use any of these preconceived categories. They can develop their own. Keep in mind that inviting students to help is time-consuming, but well worth the effort.

Establishing Levels of Performance

After the categories or domains have been selected and most elements on the conversation chart have been placed in one category or another, the group will then have to establish levels of performance for each. The easiest way to do this, if it is your first attempt at using rubrics, is to level student performance by its frequency of use. That is, you might use phrases such as "most of the time," "some of the time," "occasionally," or "rarely" to level performance.

Deciding the Number of Levels

It's probably best to start with a three-point rubric, that is, one with three levels of performance. Thus, you might select the following for your three reference points:

3 points = [Behaviors] occurred most of the time
2 points = [Behaviors] occurred some of the time
1 point = [Behaviors] occurred rarely

How might this actually play out in the classroom? Let's look at an example: Most classrooms will have included on their conversation charts: "Students look at the person speaking." The group would then have to decide into which category this rule for good conversations should be placed. It could, for example, be placed under the domain of "responsiveness" and would therefore become just one of many aspects under that domain's heading. Other aspects under the category of responsiveness might be "Every comment deserves a response" or "Listeners nodded their heads to let the speaker know they were listening." I like to actually cut the Conversation Tips chart apart into each of its elements, which then allows us to move them around at will on the floor. At any rate, once each category has several major elements under it, students will then be able to assess whether such behaviors occurred most of the time, some of the time, or only rarely. Plus, some of the traits will overlap and, thus, need to be combined or eliminated. Expect the process to be somewhat messy—but very valuable.

Organizing Our Work into a Final Form

I recommend word processing the categories, with their descriptors under them, in a manner that allows students to check off noted behaviors. It might then look something like this:

CATEGORIES	LEVEL 1 (often)	LEVEL 2 (sometimes)	LEVEL 3 (rarely)
Responsiveness			
Looked at the person speaking			√
Honored each person's response		√	
Made connections to the text			√
Made connections to other texts		√	
Participation			
Invited others to speak	√		
Stayed on each topic for awhile			√
Asked participants questions		√	

The preceding example is, of course, incomplete. It is not meant to be used as a protocol, because collaboratively constructed rubrics of every classroom will differ. This one is merely an example to present the manner in which a teacher might go about organizing the domains and their elements into a usable form.

On page 109 you will see a photographed example of one such rubric. It was created by Heidi Clarke and her fourth graders. A few students scribed the various levels of the draft while the rest brainstormed possibilities. The kids revised several times, and in the end it was all theirs. They had developed it; thus, they understood it, and it could be used effectively. However, always remember that no two classrooms will ever have identical rubrics unless the teachers collaborate and construct them together.

Developing a Metacognitive Awareness

What all of this does is develop a student's metacognitive ability; it helps her understand the process enough to be able to articulate an evaluation of conversation performance. It also does something that traditional teaching does not do: it brings that process into a describable form that can be articulated and then scaffolded into higher levels of competency. Students who are capable of describing and understanding the parts of a process are more capable of developing higher levels of performance.

*With the help of their teacher, students in Heidi Clarke's
fourth grade collaboratively develop a rough-draft
conversation rubric.*

ASSESSMENT: ROAMING OBSERVERS

A fun and easy way to monitor conversation groups is to invite one student to
serve as an observer of his group. This works best with groups larger than three,
so that removing one member does not drastically affect the richness of the conversation. However, observers can also be a member of another group (which
can be a productive activity for a student whose group members are absent). In
that case, the observers can roam from group to group, taking notes on each.

  To meet such a responsibility, one would be expected to jot down positive aspects of the observed conversations, just as the teacher modeled earlier. Note that
in the process of doing this, these students are at the same time reexperiencing
that day's reading through others' eyes. This means that although their own responses are held captive by their silent role, they will still revisit that day's reading
experience by listening to what others have to say about it and logging observations. Kids love this kind of responsibility, and I always let them know that I appreciate their contributions.

  Later, when the conversation is over and the observers have completed their
tasks, they can then become reporters to the conversation groups, as well as to

the teacher. I like to invite those students who participated in the conversation to add anything positive that they, too, may have noticed, but that *wasn't* recorded by their roaming observer. This is important because sometimes observers miss poignant aspects of the conversation, which then evokes frustration in group members. However, by including that final invitation, all voices can be heard.

To add a touch of gratitude to the procedure, I like to have small thank-yous copied and ready to hand to that day's observers. I just sign and date each one, and then invite them to take it home and share. And, although these are duplicate forms, I very often jot a special little note to each observer, making it more personal. For instance, I might write, "How did you ever notice all those things! Wow!" or "I liked the way you turned negatives into positives. Thanks!"

TRUST THE KIDS!

Any of these strategies can help teachers monitor what goes on in literature conversation triads and thereby provide a sense of security in the process. Eventually, however, the value of these conversations will be realized throughout the day and throughout the curriculum, and the teacher will no longer need to ask, "How will I know what they're doing?" For students will think more critically and creatively. They will learn to negotiate their problems and listen to others. And, every classroom interaction will become richer, thanks to in-depth experiences in literature conversations. The bottom line remains: trust the kids!

ANALYTICAL, CRITICAL, AND EVALUATIVE RESPONSES: GUIDED COMPREHENSION USING A MEANINGFUL CONTEXT

In the preceding chapters, we've used some initial steps to gain access to higher levels of response. We know that interrogatives, such as *why* and *how*, can elevate a student's level of thinking. We know that evidence-based terms, such as *because*, move thinking up a notch. And we know that a framework like the Connections Venn can help kids connect the inside world of the text to their own outside world. All of these move responders toward higher levels of thinking and thus enhance comprehension.

In this chapter, however, I want to stress the importance of connections made within a real-world, meaningful context, because in order to evaluate a text in a critical and analytical manner, kids must have experiences that are embedded in

The kids go back to the book to prove a point.

life as we live it—experiences that can be replicated in or out of school. But where do we find such critical and analytical contexts?

The Trouble with Some Texts

Often, what makes critique complicated for students can be attributed to the fine lines that exist between fact and fiction. At times this fact/fiction dilemma can confuse and baffle even adults. That is, we question those "facts" presented in the tabloids and on TV interviews. We shake our heads over biased reporting during political campaigns. And we cautiously read the fine print under "Lifetime Guarantee." It is no wonder students have difficulty understanding the shades and hues of critique.

Indeed, critique is no simple process! Whole books have been written on the topic. For now, I would like to present but one method that helped my students and others develop skill in using critical analysis and reflection, and thus gave voice and individual perspective to both their spoken and their written responses. It's an easy, real-world way to scaffold kids into the process—and they love it!

Using Book Reviews as Models for Critique

Book reviews are real-world text responses that demonstrate several levels of comprehension: determining important information, making connections, analyzing, synthesizing, and evaluating. Well-conceived book reviews usually do all this through a combination of text *summarization* and *evidenced analysis*. The good news is that there are relevant real-world reviews that we teachers can easily access—ones that hook the kids, as well. And what's more, there are places where students may actually publish reviews of their own. This solid connection to reality draws young learners to the understanding that summarization and critical analysis of text content is not just a school assessment task; it is a skill that can be used throughout life. Furthermore, they take what they've learned from reviewers and incorporate it into their own reading and writing performance.

What is a review?

Reviews always include a summary of some text, be it a book, an article, a movie, or a song—anything that can be transformed into a brief synopsis that considers the *content* of the text. However, reviews are far more than just a summary, for they have another purpose, which is to consider the *quality* of the experience that text presents. Well-written reviews incorporate both content and quality analysis and evaluation. Because they focus on quality, the best reviews therefore include personal reflection and critique, which makes them a great instructional tool. Furthermore, they are brief and come in multitudinous lots—a perfect teaching tool!

Obtaining reviews

My personal favorite review catalog and website is Chinaberry <*www.chinaberry. com*>. It is chock-full of delightful critical summaries that include first-rate review examples, many of which are presented through

- reflections related to the reviewer's own life;
- personal connections to the author's style; and
- comparisons to other texts.

Such reviews serve our purpose well, because they demonstrate the Connections Venn in action. Therefore, referencing the Venn as each review is read will help make the experience more concrete.

Certainly our Sunday newspapers and many magazines carry book reviews. Children's magazines often invite the kids themselves to contribute reviews. Furthermore, large bookstores, such as Barnes and Noble and Borders, carry monthly brochures with reviews.

I feel the most efficient book review avenue is the Internet. One of the main reasons I like that venue is because it enables us to collect reviews that have actually been written by kids. Just a few clicks and you have the reviews in hand. But, whatever you do, be sure to include a few music reviews. These are highly motivating. Kids—even the very young—love to read music reviews of their favorite recording artists. Raffi is there and so are the Backstreet Boys! The Barnes and Noble *<www.bn.com>* and Amazon *<www.amazon.com>* websites are presently two of the largest that always publish music reviews, some of which are actually written by students. (Nudge, nudge.)

Why not feed off the actual purpose of a review, which is to update and inform readers and viewers of content and quality? Students who follow the lead of the reviewer by attending a performance or by reading a book or buying a CD can later be invited to write their own review to extend the perspectives of previous reviewers. They might even like to send it in for the world to read!

Connections included in well-written reviews

It is Chinaberry that I most often lean on to show the ways in which real reviewers use higher levels of comprehending when constructing their responses. I draw the class' attention to the manner in which a review unfolds, from its (1) invitational introduction, to its (2) descriptive midsections, and on to its final (3) critical conclusions. The first and last sections usually demonstrate how the reviewer connects the text to his own world, other texts, and the craft of the author. Chinaberry reviewers do this with considerable voice. Thus, they not only teach us how to critique but also reel us in.

To begin, I try to find reviews that contain examples for each of the three connections, that is, some for life/world connections, some for other text connections, and some for author's craft connections—and it's an extra perk if the review content is related to our curriculum. I like to copy these onto reusable transparencies, rather than adding more paper to the environment. We can then view and discuss the relevant parts of each selection, highlighting or underlining the specific connection examples.

Before analyzing specific parts, we read the preselected reviews in their entirety. Chinaberry.com was kind enough to let me share the following reviews. Let's decide the kinds of connections each might offer.

The Search for Delicious
Natalie Babbitt

"Delicious" . . . that's the word for this book! It is funny, imaginative and full of subtle irony that elementary school children will love. *The Search for Delicious* involves the King's prime minister's efforts to write a dictionary. All goes well until he gets to the word "delicious." You see, everyone has a different opinion of what delicious is. The King votes for apples, the Queen is for Christmas pudding, the prime minister is for fried fish. Things go from bad to worse, and pretty soon the whole kingdom is on the verge of a civil war. With the air of a folk tale (mermaids, dwarves and woldwellers abound), *The Search for Delicious* embodies the kind of mythological symbolism children instinctively understand.

This book leads us into some wonderful discussions about the reasons why people engage in wars and about the way in which simple misunderstandings can escalate in ways no one would have ever imagined. Babbitt has made a wonderful point about how absolutely ridiculous we humans can be when we get so focused on our own ideas that we can't see the forest for the trees. This is altogether a charming book. By the way, what's your definition of delicious?

The Breadwinner

Deborah Ellis

This book sat on the top of my "to read immediately" pile of books when the shocking events of September 11, 2001 rocked the world. Suddenly what had been a distant, far off problem—the horrific treatment of people, particularly women and children, by the Taliban—was violently disturbing the peace of our lives. In *The Breadwinner*, Deborah Ellis has found just the story to elucidate the horror of the Taliban without immobilizing our children's hearts with fear. In her tale, Parvana, a young girl, is forced to masquerade as a boy to earn her family's living by reading and writing in the marketplace. Ellis deftly manages to portray the horrific and grossly violent effects the Taliban's actions bring upon the Afghani people and also show a people willing to resist and create hope in the center of horror.

The Mozart Season

Virginia Euwer Wolff

This book is about passion, about finding something that you love and devoting your heart to it. It is about finding out who you are through doing what you love, through struggling with yourself as you do what you love. On the surface, this is a story about a girl's relationship with music, with her bike, with her friends and with her world. But, in its heart, *The Mozart Season* is about developing a relationship with yourself—which, as far as I can see, is the job of every adolescent. I love this book and all the children I know who have read it have too, even the non-musicians.

Juniper

Monica Furlong

Oh, I just love it when books that I really love end up becoming part of a series. Author Monica Furlong continues weaving her magic in this prelude to *Wise Child*. This time we meet Juniper as a young girl, a girl raised with all the comforts and luxuries befitting the medieval princess that she is. Slowly through the course of various strange events, Juniper comes to recognize that she has special powers, powers that she does not understand. In seeking to understand these powers, she looks to her strange and powerful Godmother Euny for help. Though life with Euny is harsh and often unpleasant, Juniper comes to learn many important lessons which help her to understand her special talents and learn to use them for their highest good instead of for her own selfish benefit. Furlong has again created a spellbinding tale in which the characters must search their deepest selves to find the courage to respond to the challenges they face, and one in which the spiritual and the earthly mix to form one congruent pattern. Although *Wise Child* and *Juniper* are related, each stands beautifully on its own and they could easily be read in either order. Don't miss this powerful tale; it definitely satisfies the soul.

Reviews are usually rife with author's craft remarks, such as the way in which *In Search of Delicious* is described as ". . . funny, imaginative and full of subtle irony." I'd begin with an obvious connection, such as this one or *The Breadwinner*, whose connections to our lives and the world are strong and even emotional. The review of *Juniper* compares that book with another by the same author, which is a common text-to-text connection.

Investigating reviewer bias

After reading each review, I ask the students, "Does it sound like the reviewer liked the book?" Then I follow the students' responses with, "What makes you say that?" After kids have examined enough reviews, they come to realize how a writer's voice, his interests, his likes and dislikes seep through between the words.

Most book reviewers give positive reviews, so there are few examples for the opposite. However, movie reviews are far from unanimously positive. Clipping the negative reviews for a few family movies will help balance the bias scales.

A *short leap into connections*

By discussing reviews in this manner, I can not only show students how reviewers connect, summarize, and critique but carry it one step further by asking the group to link books we've read to the reviewers' connections. The kids can slide right off the reviewers' connections and onto their own. A very short leap.

INTERNALIZING ASSESSMENT AND CONNECTIONS

As students move between reviews and their own conversations, they begin to internalize the processes involved. Plus, they understand some real-world reasons for making such connections. Given the appropriate opportunities, it will happen.

For instance, by the end of the year, Sheila Delmonte's second grade had woven both connections and their assessment into each literature conversation in a natural manner. Here's a group of boys from her room who had just finished reading and discussing *Wingdingdilly* by Bill Peet. Notice how they weave connections into the assessment of their group's interactions.

Darryl: Don't you think we did piggybacking a little bit?

Mihn: We were piggybacking, and we talked quietly. We didn't disturb anybody else.

Rod: Yeah, and we didn't interrupt.

Jose: Yeah, but guys—what would that go on, like, on author's craft? Setting? Events? Characters? My life and the world?

Mihn: I think that it would go on all that because we did all that. We did all of those things. We did the characters, the setting, the author's craft—

Darryl: Even though we were stuck in one box—characters and events— we still tried to get out of that box and get into other boxes, like my life and the world and other texts.

These boys show us that not only can second graders understand how to make connections, but they can analyze their talk and articulate its merits. All students who are given literature conversation opportunities on a regular basis will also be able to do this. Incorporating guidance in assessment techniques, as well as higher-level, world-connected tasks, will surely raise performance and interest levels.

CLASSROOMS IN ACTION:
RESPONSE TRIADS USING AUTONOMOUS READING OF TEXT

Ms. Burglemeister was feeling good about the students' triad conversations. They had been responding in these small groups after her read-alouds every day for more than a week. She could tell how confident they were becoming because, first of all, they never wanted to stop when she said it was time, and furthermore, even most of the quieter students were contributing.

She noticed that conversations were becoming richer, too, and she attributed some of that to the guided comprehension strategies she presented each day during her read-alouds. She'd decided to tell the class that the first two read-aloud pages were designated as "teacher pages," through which she could demonstrate some of the things readers think about during conversations. In this way, she managed to show them how readers can question a character's intent, the author's intent, or a point of view; evaluate the text; compare the text to another text; reflect on the author's skill; and connect the text to their own lives. Each demonstration seemed to be opening up new doors to student response. Ms. Burglemeister therefore decided that today was the day—that is, it was Independence Day, the time when students would prepare for discussion by reading independently. To do this, she combined their usually unlimited-choice SSR and their reading instructional periods for the next two weeks.

The class had been studying pioneer life, so Ms. Burglemeister had acquired multiple texts by Laura Ingalls Wilder, which would allow choice within parameters. She made certain that *Little House in the Big Woods* was one of the choices because it was an easier book and would better serve her less confident readers. She called the group's attention and then invited, "Boys and girls, I have brought in the Wilder books, as I said I would. I'd like for each of you to look through all of them and decide which one you would like to read. Please remember to use the five-finger rule of reading through the first page, and if there are more than five words that you are unable to read, you should perhaps select another book. After you decide your favorites, please write your name on your index card and list your first, second, and third choices. You know that we do not have unlimited copies of each text, so I will probably have to give some of you your second or third choice. They are all good books, however, and also very similar, so we should not have any problems creating the triads."

The group was eventually divided into five triads and two quads, which took some maneuvering on the part of the teacher. But everyone seemed happy and excited to begin because they knew that they would be reading the text independently this time. So, while each group met with Ms. Burglemeister individually for prereading instruction, the others worked on a variety of independent activities in another area. Ms. Burglemeister called one group at a time to introduce vocabulary for the first chapter and to provide some schema for their reading. She was not worried about presenting the setting this time, because the class had been discussing that in social studies. They had even tracked Laura's family's journey across the country already.

After each group received this prereading instruction from their teacher, they were encouraged to begin, using during-reading sticky note responses as a mnemonic for their postreading conversation. The teacher also reminded students, "If you don't have a chance to finish the chapter today in school, remember to take it home with you tonight, so that you can participate in your conversation triad or quad tomorrow."

Everyone came prepared the next day except for Birendra, who had been absent the day before, and Bradley, who said he didn't have a chance to finish his reading. "Okay, Birendra," the teacher said, "because you weren't here, you did not have a chance to read the chapter. Do you want to participate in the conversation group anyway, rely on your triad to catch you up, and try to gather what you can from today's conversation? Or would you rather spend this time reading and catching up?"

"I'd rather go with my group," Birendra said.

"Okay. So those of you in Birendra's group, please try to remember that he has not had a chance to read, and you will need to invest a brief period filling him in. But, do not spend your whole session in summarizing the chapter for Birendra, because you also need to respond as we usually do, referencing your sticky notes."

"And, Bradley, you did not finish the chapter, right?" asked Ms. Burglemeister, somewhat seriously.

"Uh-huh," responded Bradley, without looking at the teacher.

"Well, suppose you go ahead now and finish it. And if you don't have time to participate in your group, you can respond on some notebook paper, but reference your sticky notes. And give that writing to me, please, when you are finished, so that at least *I* can respond to you. Okay?" the teacher asked.

"Okay," replied Bradley, and he went to his desk, took out his book, and began reading.

Then the teacher addressed the whole class again, "Today, while you're meeting in conversation groups, I'll be the roaming observer and jot down all the good things I see and hear happening. However, on other days I will be inviting some of you to do that because I'll be meeting with different groups throughout the conversation period in order to introduce the next chapter to each group and prepare you for your reading. So, since I can't be in two places at once, we'll need someone else to be the roaming observer."

Several students interrupted to ask if they could be the roaming observer the next day. "We'll decide when the time comes," responded Ms. Burglemeister. "But today, let's concentrate on the here and now. We want to get good at this because the camcorder is waiting to again capture exemplary conversations. I will soon be setting it up to record your groups. Hey! You'll be my star performers for next year's class!"

The students responded with smiles and excitement, asking, "When will we be taping? Tomorrow?"

"No, not tomorrow, but soon, because I know your groups will work like a charm," encouraged their teacher. "But, what we *will* be doing tomorrow is beginning to work on a way to assess conversations, so that when you finish each day, you can decide just how good you were, as well as the things you must still work on."

The Next Day

Before inviting students to meet in triads or quads to talk about their chapters, Ms. Burglemeister began, "I will soon be calling groups over to introduce the next chapter while others meet in conversation. But before I begin, I would like for all of us to work together to make a conversation assessment rubric."

"You know we've used rubrics before," the teacher went on, "but this time, I thought it would be a good idea if we tried to develop one from our conversation chart. So, I've cut apart each one of the elements that we listed, and what I'm doing now is passing them out to all of you. Some people will get more than one, but that's okay. We can work together on this."

After the cut-up chart was distributed, the teacher drew the students' attention to the front of the room, where she had placed five words across the top of the blackboard: *responsiveness*, *participation*, *clarity*, *content*, and *organization*. "Now, let me explain what each one of these means," she said, "and then I'll ask you to come up and place the descriptor you are holding under the one whose category it best matches." At that point, the teacher focused on each term, explaining its meaning and giving examples of subcategory elements.

Then she asked, "Who's ready to categorize a descriptor you're holding?" Several students raised their hands, and Ms. Burglemeister motioned for them to come to the front. She handed each a piece of masking tape and the rubric began to take shape. She continued inviting until only a few were left holding chart elements. "These may be the tough ones," the teacher suggested, "so let's all help figure them out."

Everyone worked together until all elements were on the board under some category. At that point, the teacher asked, "Does anyone see something that may have been misplaced? If so, before we move it, please explain why you think it needs to be moved."

Again the class worked together, discussing questionable placements. Eventually, everyone was able to accept all placements. "Wow!" the teacher exclaimed. "Look what we did! That was a great job! Now we can use this to keep check on how well we do each day." Ms. Burglemeister then invited triads into conversation, calling one up with her for prereading instruction on the next day's chapter. By the end of the period, all had had a chance to meet for both conversation and prereading instruction.

The Next Day

The following day the teacher had word processed the categorical chart and had also included a place to mark the performance levels, which she explained quickly and then used a transparency on the overhead projector to demonstrate how one might be marked. Afterward, she suggested, "When your group finishes today's conversation, I would like for each triad to use this three-point conversation rubric to assess how the group did today. Talk about each element, and then decide amongst yourselves at what level you feel you responded today. Look at each one and ask, 'Did we do this most of the time, some of the time, or rarely?' When you're finished, each of you should sign your name, and then hand it in to me." The class seemed excited to begin, so the teacher announced, "Okay, let's get started."

Ms. Burglemeister knew that it would be some time before the class truly understood the rubric and evaluated the elements in a realistic fashion. But, as she had said before, Rome wasn't built in a day. So, she decided to see how the groups would respond and then take it from there.

JUST KEEP ON KEEPIN' ON

Once students get to this point in the process, all that's left to do is to just keep on keepin' on; that is, keep modeling, keep calling the circle and inviting partner and triad conversations, keep searching for more connections, keep reading rich texts, keep assessing the process.

Just two last reminders: Trust the kids! And, let *them* ask the questions!

AFTERWORD
THE ERIC STORY

In conversation, we practice good human behaviors. We think, we laugh, we cry, we tell stories of our day. We become visible to one another. We gain insights and new understandings. And as we stay in conversation, we may discover that we want to be activists in our world. We get interested in what we can do to change things. Conversation wakes us up. We no longer accept being treated poorly. We become people who work to change our situation.
Margaret Wheatley, Turning to One Another (2002, 140)

It seems like Meg Wheatley wrote this for Eric. His is a story that can happen afterward, that is, after we offer our students venues for voice.

You see, the whole conversation process is *really* about more than just literature and comprehension. It's about finding one's voice. It's about discovering who we are. It's about taking a stand—one which, in turn, inspires the compelling, almost obsessive urge to act, to do something. Indeed, it's about overcoming voiceless complacency. Conversations are about becoming the kind of citizen that will actively sustain America as a democracy, which *should* be the number one standard in every classroom in this country.

Literature conversations prepare young people for becoming active, dedicated, voiceful citizens. They help kids move beyond "Here is what I know . . ." to "Here is how I can use what I know. . . ." Kids evolve from just talking about pollution to doing something about it, from just talking about abuse to doing something about it, from just talking about democracy to using the privileges that citizenship offers—starting with the First Amendment. Even kids eventually learn that: "Reality doesn't change itself. It needs us to act" (Wheatley 2002, 27).

Eric, one of my former students, discovered this. His kindergarten teacher informed me, "Ardie, Eric has not talked all year. I hope he will come out of his shell in first grade." That next year Eric had lots of opportunities to test his voice when he interacted in myriad literature conversations, and at the year's end, Eric even participated in a conversation circle in front of 550 teachers at that year's Whole Language Umbrella convention in Niagara Falls. Eric was definitely out of his shell.

However, that is not the end of the story. Eric became energized also by our units of study, one of which involved the plight of the whales within a deteriorating environment. After reading related books and articles, he and a small group of his peers, as well as a senior citizen volunteer, discussed and then developed, signed, and sent a letter to a congressman—a letter that took the united stance of an informed group of citizens.

However, that is not the end of the story. The following year Eric grew interested (at home) in a group that supported whale adoption, and when one of its newsletters explained former President Clinton's obvious complacency regarding the issue, Eric again wrote to his congressman. He explained the issue as he saw it and asked Congressman LaFalce to contact the president, imploring, "Don't you *care* about the whales?"

Congressman LaFalce answered Eric's letter and then passed it on to President Clinton. However, this young activist grew impatient waiting for some kind of action, and therefore put the pen to the page again. This time he wrote to Raffi, the children's entertainer and activist who wrote and sang the whale song "Baby Beluga." Eric explained the problem to this kindred spirit and asked him to use his influence and write to the president and the vice president. "I thought Al Gore loved the whales," Eric explained, "because he wrote *Earth in Balance* [a book that Eric encountered during our first-grade ecology unit]."

Thus, Raffi, who understands the importance of a child's voice, as well as the plight of the whales, wrote back to this now third grader. However, Raffi also wrote to President Clinton "on Eric's behalf," and then sent Eric a copy of that letter.

However, the story does not end there, either, because soon afterward, Eric received a letter from President Clinton himself, assuring this young activist that he, too, loved the whales. He provided Eric with lots of information, but in the end committed to nothing. When Eric received the president's letter, he sat down and wrote a thank-you to everyone; however, midway through his letter of appreciation to Mr. LaFalce, this third grader explained that, although he appreciated their responses, he also understood that the president had taken no real action, had made no actual commitment. Thus, Eric asked again, "When *is* President Clinton going to do something?" And he underlined the word "is" to further make his point.

However, the story doesn't end there, either. Actually, the story will never end. Eric's voice, Eric's passions, Eric's knowledge did not develop overnight— nor did they develop on the pages of a workbook or in test preparation activities.

This kind of passion takes root in classrooms that sow opportunities for voice. Through literature conversations, Eric learned his voice would be heard and responded to. In studying animals and the environment, he learned that some-one had better speak up. And he spoke up because he had had experience with his voice being heard and respected. The experience was real. The issues were real. His response to them: real.

In the aftermath of literature conversations and other "Eric stories," I have grown to understand that each book talk is actually a practice of freedom. When we are caught up in conversation's individual pieces and parts, it's sometimes dif-ficult to envision the whole and its implications. I now understand that each con-versation will be shaded by difference, yet each will also be hued by sameness. That sameness is the spirit of freedom that shines from each small piece, each step, so much so that the whole, indeed, becomes greater than its parts. And there, we have the formula for passion.

May the threads of literature conversation weave voice and passion into your classroom, as together, we create a beautiful tapestry of neverending Eric stories.

APPENDIX 1
BIBLIOGRAPHY OF
READ-ALOUD BOOKS

The following read-aloud books offer a broad palate of topics, genres, and styles. What they have in common is their impetus to evoke wonderment. After all, creating the soil to nurture wonder is our purpose here.

I have not leveled these books because I do not believe there is a grade level I could attach to any of them. I would read 90 percent of them to primary-age students, knowing that, when their topics are complex or foreign, their power to evoke wonders will be that much greater. Furthermore, students' listening levels are higher than their independent reading levels. Plus, they are picture books, which means students have more context with which to construct their knowledge.

The majority of these books could be read to students repeatedly throughout the elementary grades, and each time, different questions would be evoked. The reason for this is because most of these selections evoke questions that have no one right answer. Thus, we wonder and we wonder and we wonder. And in the end, it all becomes the perfect grist for rich conversation.

Altman, L. J., and C. VanWright, illus. 2000. *The Legend of Freedom Hall*. New York: Lee & Low.

Baillie, A., and J. Tanner, illus. *Drac and Gremlin*. New York: Penguin Books.

Baker, K. 1989. *The Magic Fan*. New York: Harcourt Brace.

Bilder, P., and C. F. Payne, illus. 2002. *Shoeless Joe and Black Betsy*. New York: Simon & Schuster.

Bond, K. G., and D. Tate, illus. 2001. *The Legend of the Valentine*. Grand Rapids, MI: Zonderkidz.

Bunting, E., and C. Soentpiet, illus. 2001. *Jin Woo*. New York: Clarion.

Cherry, L. 1992. *The River Ran Wild*. New York: Harcourt.

———. 2000. *The Great Kapok Tree: The Tale of the Amazon Forest*. New York: Harcourt.

Choi, Y. 2001. *The Name Jar*. New York: Knopf.

Demi. 2000. *The Emporer's New Clothes*. New York: Simon & Schuster.

Dewey, J. O. 2000. *Rattlesnake Dance: True Tales, Mysteries, and Rattlesnake Ceremonies*. New York: Boyds Mills.

George, J. C., and W. Minor. 2002. *Cliff Hanger*. New York: HarperCollins.

Gerstein, M. 1998. *The Wild Boy*. New York: Farrar, Strauss, & Giroux.

Goble, P. 1978. *The Girl Who Loved Wild Horses*. New York: Simon & Schuster.

Heide, F. P., and J. H. Gilliland, illus. 1992. *Sami and the Time of the Troubles*. New York: Clarion.

Hoban, R., and I. Andrew, illus. *Jim's Lion*. Cambridge, MA: Candlewick Press.

Hodges, M. 1995. *Gulliver in Lilliput*. New York: Holiday House.

Hodges, M., and T. S. Hyman, illus. 1996. *Comus* (or *Childe Roland*). New York: Holiday House.

Hopkinson, D., and J. E. Ransome. 2002. *Under the Quilt of Night*. New York: Simon & Schuster.

Howard, A., and S. Wells, illus. *The Great Wonder*. Washington, DC: Trudy Corporation & Smithsonian Institute.

Kenan, K., and P. Catalanotto, illus. 2002. *The Dream Shop*. New York: HarperCollins.

Kipling, R. 1986. *The Elephant's Child*. New York: Knopf.

Kroll, S., and M. Chesworth, illus. 1994. *Doctor on an Elephant*. New York: Holt.

Lamorisse, A. 1956. *The Red Balloon*. New York: Bantam Doubleday.

Levy, J., and N. Levy. 1994. *There Are Those*. New York: NL Associates.

Lewis, P. O. 1995. *Storm Boy*. Berkley, CA: Tricycle Press.

Lightburn, S., and R. Lightburn. 1998. *Driftwood Cove*. Toronto: Doubleday.

McGugan, J., and M. Kimber, illus. 1994. *Josepha: A Prairie Boy's Story*. San Francisco: Chronicle Books.

Macauley, D. 1979. *Motel of Mysteries*. New York: Aker.

Martin, R., and D. Shannon, illus. 1992. *The Rough-Faced Girl*. New York: G. P. Putnam's Sons.

Medina, T., and R. G. Christie, illus. 2002. *Love to Langston*. New York: Lee & Low.

Miles, M., and P. Parnell, illus. 1985. *Annie and the Old One*. Chicago: Scott Foresman.

Mochizuki, K., and D. Lee, illus. 1997. *Passage to Freedom: The Sugihara Story*. New York: Lee & Low.

Muth, J. J. 2002. *The Three Questions: Based on a Story by Leo Tolstoy*. New York: Scholastic.

Paulus, T. 1972. *Hope for the Flowers*. New York: Aker.

Pinkney, A. D., and B. Pinkney. 2002. *Ella Fitzgerald: The Tale of Vocal Virtuosa*. New York: Hyperion Books.

Polacco, P. 1998. *Thank You, Mr. Falker*. New York: Philomel Books.

Rand, G., and T. Rand, illus. 1992. *Prince William*. New York: Holt.

Rockwell, A., and R. G. Christie. 2000. *Only Passing Through: The Story of Sojourner Truth*. New York: Knopf.

Say, A. 1999. *Tea with Milk*. Boston: Houghton Mifflin.

———. 2002. *Home of the Brave*. Boston: Houghton Mifflin.

Sheldon, D., and G. Blythe, illus. 1997. *The Whale's Song*. New York: Viking.

Silverstein, S. 1964. *The Giving Tree*. New York: HarperCollins.

Thien, M. 2001. *The Chinese Violin*. Vancouver: Whitecap Books.

Van Allsburg, C. 1979. *The Garden of Abdul Gasazi*. New York: Clarion.

———. 1981. *Jumanji*. New York: Clarion.

———. 1983. *The Wreck of the Zephyr*. New York: Clarion.

———. 1984. *The Mysteries of Harris Burdick*. New York: Clarion.

———. 1985. *The Polar Express*. New York: Clarion.

———. 1986. *The Stranger*. New York: Clarion.

———. 1988. *Two Bad Ants*. New York: Clarion.

———. 1990. *Just a Dream*. New York: Clarion.

———. 1991. *The Wretched Stone*. New York: Clarion.

———. 1992. *The Widow's Broom*. New York: Clarion.

———. 1997. *Ben's Dream*. New York: Clarion.

Williams, S. A., and C. Byard, illus. 1992. *Working Cotton*. New York: Harcourt Brace Jovanovich.

Yolen, J., and E. Young, illus. 1987. *The Girl Who Loved the Wind*. New York: HarperTrophy.

Zolotow, C. 1985. *William's Doll*. New York: HarperTrophy.

APPENDIX 2
TRANSCRIPTIONS FROM LITERATURE CONVERSATIONS

The following transcriptions were taken from a variety of videos taped during classroom literature conversations in every elementary grade. They may be reproduced to allow students experiences in investigating the nuts and bolts of the process. Throughout *Knee to Knee, Eye to Eye*, suggestions were made incorporating their use; however, there will be many other situations that might call for their use. You will quickly come to realize that kids love this critical, investigative experience—which, of course, still works best if it is kept positive. The ongoing question remains: "What do you see that is making this conversation work?"

Example 1 from
The Great Kapok Tree

Zula: I didn't understand why he dropped his axe.

Tenisha: Because he didn't want to bring his axe because that would remind him to chop it down.

Willow: I think because he changed his mind and said, "I don't wanta to chop that tree down."

Tenisha: Look, look [*pointing at someone coming in*].

Willow: Okay, but we're not talking about that.

Tenisha: I know, we're getting off topic.

Willow: I wonder why he slept [*pointing to picture*].

Tenisha: Because! He was very sleepy from chopping that hard tree down 'cause it wouldn't fall [*making chopping motions*].

Tula: Yeah, see that. Look at this tree [*pointing to it*]. If you turn the page, this page, you can see. [*She leans across the table to help her peer find the page.*]

Tenisha: 'Cause the bark is so hard and thin that you have to cut right through it 'cause it's so hard [*making motions*].

Vinnie: Yeah, you could get—

Tenisha: And it can't come down 'cause it's so old.

Tula: If it was up here [*pointing*] it could fall down.

Tenisha: But since it's up here, it can't come down. Its bark has been there for a long time.

Willow: Could you let me talk, please? Why is he sleeping on that ground? Maybe there's an ant that could sting him.

Tula: Some ants don't sting.

Tenisha: The bees were just trying to talk to him, because he was gonna chop down the tree.

Vinnie: Yeah, but I think he needed some rest because this is as hard as a rock.

Willow: Why can't he sleep over here [*pointing*]?

Tenisha:	Because there's a leopard on the branch.
Tula:	Yeah, and some leopards eat people.
Vinnie:	Yeah, leopards eat people. And some leopard seals eat people.
Tenisha:	*No they don't!*
Vinnie:	Yeah.
Tenisha:	No. Seals don't eat people!
Tula:	We're getting off the topic.
Lynn:	Why's the boy butt naked?
Tula:	Yeah, why's the boy butt naked?
Tenisha:	Yeah, why's he got butt naked?
Vinnie:	Yeah, why is the boy butt naked?
Tenisha:	We don't even know why.
Vinnie:	I don't understand this page because animals are crowding him [*pointing*] and the boy hid behind the tree.
Willow:	Yeah, because the animals don't want the guy to cut the tree.
Tula:	Let Lynn go.
Tenisha:	No, she already went.
Tula:	Yeah, she didn't get a lot of turns though.
Vinnie:	Lynn only had one turn.

Example 2 from
Mr. Popper's Penguins

Zack: Is this a storybook or a real book?

Michael: Storybook.

Jennifer: No, it says [*reading from back cover*] "Mr. Popper was a house-painter." [*She sits back and drops the book into her lap*.] That means it's true—

Crystal: [*breaks in reading from back cover*] She wrote this book?

Kyla: No, it says back here [*looking at back cover*]. Look! [*pointing to a specific part*] On the back it tells about the book.

Jennifer: I didn't hear.

Crystal: Want me to tell you? Okay, I'll just give out the secret. The guy that is over in Antarctica gives him penguins.

Jennifer: You gave us the secret [*teasingly frustrated*]!

Michael: Well, I was reading it anyway.

Kyla: But, look, right here, you guys [*pointing to the back again*]— you can't be reading this to see if it's a true story or not—it just *tells* about the book!

Jennifer: I was wondering how 432 Proudfoot Avenue could be the same as Mr. Popper's house and their own house—

Kyla: Yeah? That's right—oh! They're on a street.

Michael: I didn't know it said they're living on a—

Jennifer: Yeah, they're on a street—I think.

Michael: [*clarifying again*] They're *living* on that street.

Jennifer: No, it said in here that 432 Proudfoot Ave. is the—uh, uh—is the same thing that, that picture is about, and that uh—

Michael: Maybe, uh, maybe there is two names for one street, maybe—

Jennifer: We got a name for *our* street.

Crystal: How 'bout if we—let's write [*looking at front cover of book*] to the—uh, Richard and Florence Ashwater [*the authors*] and see if—

Jennifer:	Maybe they're dead, and ya can't write to 'em—
Kyla:	Oh, they might be dead.
Jennifer:	What if they died? Yeah, they might be dead.
Crystal:	Yeah, but look-it. Listen to this [*turning to the copyright page again*]. Look at this, okay?
Kyla:	Oh, yeah, it says right here, "Copyright"!
Crystal:	"Copyright renewed 1960 by Florence Atwater, Doris Atwater, and Carroll Atwater—"
Zach:	They're too old *now* [*with finality!*].
Kyla:	'60s? It says 1960s? Hm-m.
Crystal:	Look at this. Listen to this: [*She reads the entire "All right reserved" information from the copyright page of the book.*]
Others:	[*All look at Crystal questioningly.*]
Crystal:	So-o-o-o—
Jennifer:	Yeah, but, well, what're we gonna say?
Crystal:	Is Mr. Popper's Penguins a real story or not?
Jennifer:	Well, maybe—what if, what if—
Kyla:	Why don't we write to him and ask him if it's a true story or not?
Crystal:	Yeah, that is what I was trying to prove.

Example 3 from
Matilda

Anna:	I wonder why the mom and dad have to have a special shampoo.
Jennie:	Well, because their hair is a different color and they want it to be the color that they like.
Anna:	Yeah, like, they want their work to be good, and to have, like, good hairs and everything.
Delanie:	Yeah, 'cause they're rich and stuff.
Anna:	Well, they're not really rich, or anything. They just care about themselves sometimes.
Ellie:	Well, they are kinda rich because his dad gets a lot of money from the cars and stuff.
Delanie:	Yeah.
Anna:	Yeah, like two hundred dollars!
Jennie:	Because he cheats!
Girls:	Yeah!
Anna:	Why is Matilda only in kindergarten and she's doing her multiplying facts.
Jennie:	Because, you know, she reads a lot. And she got those multiplying facts.
Tiana:	No, she means that why is her teacher telling her to multiply and stuff.
Anna:	And they're only in kindergarten!
Jennie:	I know, she wants her to learn—
Delanie:	Yeah, 'cause Matilda raised her hand, you know, and she was saying a lot of multiplying facts, and the teacher was trying to test check to see if she could get, like, every one she could think of right.
Tiana:	I can't believe that Matilda read 411 pages in one week when she was only four years old.
Jennie:	She started—

134

Ellie:	Well, she started when she was one and a half, so—
Girls:	Yeah.
Anna:	And she was, like, hiding all these books, so—
Jennie:	She, she might of started reading, like, a little faster.
Tiana:	I wonder why she always [unclear].
Anna:	Well, because she's a really smart kid, and if she learns a lot, and—
Jennie:	Then how would she know all this?
Tiana:	Well, she was just born with, uh, with magic.
Anna:	Yeah, she was born, like, a really smart girl.
Girls:	Yeah.
Anna:	I wonder, what does the word *quivering* means?
Jennie:	Scared? Shaking?
Tiana:	I wondered the same thing.
Ellie:	I don't know what that word means. I never read that before.
Tiana:	I wonder why Matilda's parents are not glad that Matilda is so smart.
Ellie:	All they care about, they care about only their sons and their selves. They're very rude parents.
Anna:	Yeah, because they only like the TV, and they don't wanta really—
Jennie:	Yeah, and they only like older—
Anna:	They don't really want—all they want is to, like, watch TV and not do anything else.
Ellie:	Yeah, but she likes reading—
Jennie:	Every afternoon—
Tiana:	And, they only have TV dinners.
Jennie:	Every afternoon she sneaks around—
Tiana:	I wonder why they call the TV "the tellie."
Anna:	[*laughing*] Yeah, really!
Ellie:	Probably because they watch TV so much.

Jennie:	Or maybe they watch the show that's called *The TV Tellie.*
Ellie:	Or maybe they watch *Teletubbies* or something.
Jennie:	I don't think they had *Teletubbies* back then.
Tiana:	It wouldn't be back then, because it's not a true story.
Girls:	Oh, yeah—
Tiana:	They didn't have *Teletubbies* back then. Or, maybe they did.
Ellie:	I wondered how her dad's hair got so [unclear].
Anna and *Jennie:*	Because she put her—
Anna:	Because she put her mom's hair into her dad's hair that he uses—
Jennie:	She mixed it.
Anna:	And he mixed it up, she shook it so he couldn't see the color.
Tiana:	I wonder how the glue was, got stuck on his hair, but not—
Anna:	Because it was like super, super glue and—
Ellie:	And it dries like in a flash [*clicking her fingers for emphasis*].
Ellie:	Yeah, so they tried to, they were trying to yank it off, and it dried in, like, five minutes, you know?
Jennie:	They yanked it [unclear].
Tiana:	But they didn't because the hair just came off [*laughing*].
Girls:	[*Laughing*] Yeah.
Ellie:	Yeah, that's why they had to cut his hair.
Tiana:	I wonder what "second-hand cars" means.
Anna:	Well, very fashioned cars, like—
Jennie:	Yeah, like old-fashion stuff—
Anna:	Yeah, like a old junky stuff—
Ellie:	Yeah.

136

Jennie:	I'm wondering why Miss Honey is so fragile, 'cause people—
Anna:	She's very gentle and everything.
Jennie:	She's not like the principal, you know—
Anna:	Yeah, 'cause, like, her aunt is principal and she, like, really hurt Matilda and she doesn't want to be like that so she's very gentle and everything.
Tiana:	That's weird how Miss Trenchbow is an aunt to, uh, uh, Miss Honey, and she's a teacher, too, or a principal.
Anna:	[*screwing up her nose in distaste*] Yeah!
Jennie:	She's, like, she's, like, really mean.
Tiana:	That would be weird that she's the aunt of, like, a nice child.
Ellie:	Well, probably when she was young she would treat her very nice, but when she was older she was meaner, 'cause some people are mean when they are older.
Jennie:	But now she just doesn't like children, and that's why—
Tiana:	And I remember when Miss Honey went into Miss Trenchbow's office and uh—
Ellie:	She shoulda gone—
Tiana:	And Miss Honey told Miss Trenchbow that Matilda should go in a higher grade and Miss Trenchbow thought that she was, that Miss Honey was saying that she was a little brat—
Jennie:	She didn't know what she was saying—
Anna:	Yeah, she didn't know that she really liked her and that she was a really smart kid. And Miss Trenchbow thought she was a little bratty and evil and stuff.
Jennie:	Yeah, and she wouldn't believe it 'cause she was rushing and stuff.
Ellie:	Yeah, and 'cause her parents aren't really smart at all.
Jennie:	Yeah, and if her parents told Miss Trenchbow to blame everything on her it wouldn't be fair because everyone would, except Lavender.
Ellie:	Yeah, everyone's, like, mean to her except Miss Honey.

Tiana:	Yeah, I know Miss Honey's not mean.
Ellie:	And Lavender.
Tiana:	Yeah, Lavender. And so was that other girl. That big girl?
Jennie:	Oh yeah. The one who eats a lot?
Ellie:	And you know her friend, Brett?
Jennie:	Uh-huh.
Ellie:	That's one of them.
Tiana:	You know the two girls who eat a lot and the boy who had to eat that chocolate cake.
Girls:	Oh yeah [*laughing*].

Example 4 from
Roll of Thunder, Hear My Cry

Lasandra: I wonder what Mr. Hammond is gonna do about his sons.

Maretta: I don't know. Maybe hurt them or something.

Joey: Yeah, 'cause he was talking about a gun in there.

Lasandra: Yeah!

Lasandra: I wonder why he brings a gun when he's going for Christmas. Why would he need a *gun* when it's Christmas?

Maretta: Well, because maybe if he really goes there and they might try and hurt him.

Joey: Yeah, because—

Lasandra: Yeah, because they're gonna hurt him before—

Maretta: Yeah—

Lasandra: Yeah, because he pushed Cass on the road and that.

Joey: Maybe they're in the war with him there, 'cause they're really mean to him.

Lasandra: No—

Joey: Yeah, he's been in the war—

Lasandra: 'Cause he said his leg got blown off—

Joey: *Almost* blown off!

Maretta: Oh-h-h! Maybe Mr. Simms will wanta—

Joey: Try to pull his leg off—

Maretta: Yeah! That's why he was limping. It said in the book he was limping. It was his left leg.

Lasandra: [*reading*]"Standing firmly on his left leg."

Joey: Yeah! Okay now, I wonder what Big Ma means by "That's just the way."

Maretta: That means, like, they—'member a long, long time ago when there was blacks? Remember, he had to do all the white people before he did the black people?

139

Joey:	Yeah, like Stacy said, "You just don't understand."
Lasandra:	It's like—
Joey:	She could have got burnt.
Lasandra:	I don't really understand, first in the beginning, "Oh we don't need Mr. Morrison. I could do all that stuff he does." But, uh, Mr. Morrison does all this work. I don't know why he's so quiet.
Joey:	You know why?
Lasandra:	But, like he's quiet. It's so weird. Like when he says he'll leave it up to Stacy, and, like, they went up to the wall store that his mom doesn't allow them to. Then he had to go up and beat up—
Joey:	Yeah, and most of the time he's not at his cabin, 'cause they said in the book—
Lasandra:	Yeah, he's working—he's working—
Joey:	No, I think that he's probably doing work trying to—like, he's liking the white people—
Maretta:	Or maybe he's trying to find a plan to, like—get rid of the white people to—like, stop the war.
Lasandra:	For some reason he's getting all other white kids, men.
Maretta:	I know. He should be, like, just calling them normal names, it's like—they're just all grown up like a big person—
Lasandra:	I know—
Joey:	No! They don't call kids that.
Lasandra:	No, 'cause Miss Lillian Jean is a kid.
Maretta:	Yeah, they're kids.
Joey:	No, they're—
Maretta:	Yeah, they're like little girls. They're like eighteen-year-olds.
Joey:	No—they're like—
Lasandra:	Cassie's in fourth grade.
Joey:	Yeah, so they're, like, in their twenties.
Lasandra:	Lillian Jean—
Maretta:	Yeah, they are in their twenties. Because they still live with their father.

Lasandra:	Why would they live with their father if they were—
Joey:	Sometimes when you're still twenty, you still live with them!
Lasandra:	I know, but they're maybe nineteen.
Joey:	No, they're twenty.
Lasandra:	They aren't even teenagers yet, you guys!
Maretta:	Okay then. Eleven.
Joey:	No-o-o!
Lasandra:	Okay, they could be eleven. I think it said in the book that Cassie's nine or ten. Yeah, she's ten.
Joey:	No, because, like, even, like, when you're twenty, someone would do some of that—
Lasandra:	Yeah, but they're still kids. Our age. They're not twenty, they're our age.

Example 5 from
Toliver's Travels

Nala: I wonder what the message said. Like, maybe the message is about something that's gonna happen.

Lucia: Well, when was this taking place?

Sim: About the time of the Revolution because it's one of the—it says, like, somewhere in here that the father died—

Asa: And it's probably some time when they're not ending the war, because if the redcoats are in their house, then—

Sim: I was wondering about the girl.

Lucia: Yeah, she looks beat.

Darien: She's like a bully!

Lucia: Who is Dicey?

Asa: Maybe she's an orphan.

Sim: It's on page—

Sim: She just looks—she fits the description and her hair [*looking at a picture*] and all, I think she's having a hard time in her life.

Lucia: She might even be an English spy or something.

Sim: Yeah, and I was also wondering—

Holly: But, if she was, she wouldn't be living with them.

Sim: That's a good point. I think maybe she's just having a hard time.

Holly: I think she should do more than just—

Asa: I think she should get to her mom, even though it's kind of—

Sim: Yeah, but sometimes if you tell someone they usually come, and I think, like, she doesn't want—and I think, like, she has a really bad reputation at this point because everybody's like: "Oh, has Dicey been to this well?"

Darien: Yeah, and she doesn't want to go there because they might do that.

Sim: Yeah, and her grandfather had bought water before, but her grandfather, he could—

142

Example 6 from
Number the Stars

Lois:	That part was a little surprising. Like, I said, "What're they gonna do with the handkerchief?" Like, is he gonna blow his nose on it or something?
Others:	[*laughing*]
Rowena:	Yeah, that was confusing.
Lois:	What they do in the book is—like, I've read a couple of books and what they'll do is they'll tell you what's going on—something that they didn't tell the character, or something like that. But, in this book they just left you hanging, and so, right when you think—
Nigel:	Actually, they *told* the character—
Lois:	Uh-huh, right, I know, but they get you hooked because you gotta find out what's gonna happen.
Rowena:	Yeah, it's kind of like they're expecting us, and we're like, um-m-m, and don't really get what's going on.
Liz:	It's gonna help us with the afterwards, because of all the information. It cleared it up and we weren't very confused.
Mona:	I got one. In the first [unclear], I'm surprised she didn't argue with them. She says, like [*laughing*], "I'd rather be a nurse."
Lois:	Yeah [*laughing*].
Liz:	Yeah, because she was thinking, like, it's says—[*She starts to read from the book but gets interrupted.*]
Lois:	It's like, "I'm gonna be a nurse so I can take care of Momma," and it was really kind of funny.
Liz:	She's still kind of shy.
Nigel:	Yeah, but she started looking out for her own self.
Liz:	But she sometimes does act like a little child. By the time she—
Lois:	She *was* a child.
Liz:	[*laughing*] Well, I know, but—
Lois:	You mean like smaller?

Liz:	Yeah, I'm surprised by her, because she's kind of maturing, and I think she's kind of getting what's going on. Like, what's kind of happening. 'Cause there's so much stuff going on.
Lois:	I think she's kind of learning things by herself. She's sort of—
Liz:	Figuring out—
Lois:	Yeah, figuring out.
Liz:	Like, the missing pieces to a puzzle or something.
Lois:	Yeah, she thinks she's a little bit more mature than a normal five-year-old would be, because she's kind of keeping things to herself. She seems like the kind of person that would kind of keep things to herself sometimes.
Liz:	Uh-huh. Does anyone have something? [*looking around the circle to move on*]
Liz:	On 174, I was wondering where are they getting the boats all the time, because I mean if they went so fast, like them and, like, she just got there and he just left, like, what? Two hours before?
Liz:	I thought that was a good idea for him to ask the scientist about the dogs, like, that was really clever, would there be ways to get the dogs so that they don't get the scent. But I was surprised because I was just wondering this while I was reading: what if the scientist was German, and he didn't know that? I was just wondering what would the scientist do if they asked him that because he might give him the wrong information or something. Because that would be kind of scary because that would change the whole topic of the story.
Lois:	On 124 what do they mean by [unclear]?
Nigel:	Remember the baby medicine? So it wouldn't wake up and cry?
Rowena:	They gave the baby drugs because the lady's like—
Nigel:	Remember if the baby wakes up and cries and then the soldier stops on board—
Lois:	Yeah, I know it had something to do with, like, I didn't know what it meant, like, did they give it medicine or did they, like, hide her someplace or something like that—
Mona:	Because remember, he put, they put—someone was sleeping?
Lois:	He what?
Mona:	He put "our baby is sleeping in the house."

Lois:	He did that?
Nigel:	In the message.
Lois:	Oh-h-h-h!
Nigel:	Yeah because, remember, the mother didn't want him or something.
Liz:	I was wondering why he was giving the baby sleeping medicine because the soldiers already came.
Lois:	And the only part that we knew about was that he was going on a long fishing trip.
Rowena:	I thought that was funny when she said about the god of thunder following on the path.
Lois:	Yeah, she said [*reading*] "'Look,' she pointed, 'the god of thunder is following Pinocchio'." I think that's a funny way for a cat to be—
Nigel:	It's a kitten!
Liz:	That was funny when she said, "The godfather left rain in the corner."
All:	[*laughter*]
Lois:	It's such a good book—
Liz:	They just find good things to relate to.
Lois:	Yeah! Okay, let's go on. Who has one?
Rowena:	I put "Yea! They finally got freedom!"
Lois:	It was a really sweet ending for the book.
Liz:	She's a good author.
Lois:	Yeah, the story was, like, really, really good, and, like, it kept you hanging and everything, but in the end, they got away.
Liz:	Because most people don't know how to relate to that because at first they kind of confuse you, but they didn't really do that throughout the whole book.
Lois:	Right, they cleared things up in certain parts. It made so much more sense. And, with everything that happened in the book, you were able to go back and it would explain everything.
Liz:	You know, I said [*checking her sticky note*], "Why did they kill Peter?" He's not Jewish.

Lois:	He was protecting everybody. He didn't *have* to be Jewish.
Liz:	I know, but you know how they said that he was protecting people, well wouldn't everyone else be killed too along with him?
Mona:	They captured him.
Liz:	They only captured *him*?
Nigel:	Because they found this confederation he was a part of, and so—
Liz:	But I mean this happened *before*!
Mona:	It was two years after this was.
Lois:	Because he had written a letter. It was two years after. It said [*reading*], "He had written a letter to him on the night he was shot, and simply said that he loved them and that he was not afraid and that he was proud to have done what he could do for his country and for the sake of all the people." So, he had been helping the people out, and the Nazis found out—
Liz:	So that's why!
Lois:	Right, so he was helping people get—
Liz:	Yeah, they just said that he was happy that he did that but they didn't quite say why. They just said whether he got captured or not.
Nigel:	They actually buried everybody they saw helping him do it.
Lois:	It said, "He simply buried them when they were killed and marked the graves only with numbers." Obviously, there was more than just Peter.
Liz:	Uh-huh. There was so much numbers.
Mona:	How did they know which number Peter was if they went back to visit him? They said that—
Liz:	Oh, yeah, 'cause that's—
Mona:	They said they went back—
Liz:	It said [*reading*]: "Annemarie had gone to the place with her parents . . . on the numbered ground." Maybe they asked the people.
Lois:	Maybe they put flowers on *everybody's* grave, because they *all* tried to help with every situation and all, so maybe they wanted to thank *everybody*. So, they gave everybody a flower.

Mona:	Uh-huh.
Lois:	On page 129 I thought it was sad because—I thought it was sad that Peter had died and everything because he was doing good things for everybody.
Nigel:	He died for—
Lois:	Also, though, Kirsti was taking things seriously. I mean, I know she was getting older and everything, but now everything is, like, coming to her.
Nigel:	It's like, it's like the war changed her.
All:	Uh-huh.
Lois:	Made things, like, a whole lot different.
Rowena:	Yeah, but I mean, wait! Remember when they said, like, "Oh, weren't there fireworks?"
Liz:	But then, later they said it was actually explosions.
Lois:	Uh-huh.
Liz:	So then, actually, her mom just didn't want to scare her.
All:	Uh-huh.
Liz:	And who would want to know that!
Nigel:	Yeah, and remember how her mom kept saying, "Some things you don't have to know and it would be better for you"?
Liz:	I think that if you're really young, like only four years old, and so much is, like, happening, you know? Then I really wouldn't want to know. Because Kirsti, she thought it out by herself. I think maybe it was a lot easier for her to figure it out, because it was the right time for her to find out instead of her mom telling her. And I think it was the same thing with Annemarie, how her uncle said it was safer for you not to know.
Lois:	Uh-huh, now I'm just gonna go back to something we talked about a few minutes ago. It's a good thing that Kirsti was very, very smart, because remember when the soldiers stopped her on the corner and she said, "Don't! Don't touch my hair!" and everything like that?
Mona:	And she distracted them.
Liz:	Oh-h-h-h.

Lois:	Right, and it was kind of a good thing that Kirsti wasn't being so mature at that point.
Liz:	Well, she kind of was, because maybe she was feeling like—
Lois:	Yeah, but then Annemarie thought, "Well, what would Kirsti have done?" So, it was kind of a good thing that Kirsti wasn't trying to grow up really, really fast because she wouldn't have thought of anything like that. And, I think it is pretty much the other way around. You know how many times Kirsti looks up to Annemarie, well I think it's the other way around: Annemarie looks up to Kirsti a lot.
Nigel:	Yeah.
Liz:	Yeah, like when the soldiers came, she kept saying, "What would Kirsti do? What would Kirsti do?" And, if Kirsti didn't do that, Annemarie wouldn't have known what to do. So, it was kind of a bad thing, but in a way, it was a good thing.
Mona:	I got one. Well, before we found out how Peter died, I was *really, really* wondering *how* he died.
Liz:	Yeah, because they didn't really talk about how he died.
Nigel:	It didn't tell you how he died till the end of the book.

REFERENCES

CHILDREN'S BOOKS

Atwater, R., and F. Atwater. 1938. *Mr. Popper's Penguins*. New York: Dell.

Cherry, L. 2000. *The Great Kapok Tree*. New York: Harcourt.

Cleary, B. *Ramona and the Mystery Meal and Rainy Sunday*. Irvine, CA: Lorimar Films.

Crews, D. 1978. *Freight Train*. New York: Puffin.

Dahl, R., and Q. Blake. 1998. *Matilda*. New York: Puffin.

Gannett, R. S. 1948. *My Father's Dragon*. New York: Trumpet Book Club.

George, J. C. 1988. *My Side of the Mountain*. New York: Puffin.

Kraus, R., and J. Aruego, 1970. *Whose Mouse Are You?* New York: Macmillan.

Lowry, L. 1989. *Number the Stars*. New York: Bantam Doubleday Dell.

Patterson, K. 1987. *The Great Gilly Hopkins*. New York: HarperTrophy.

Sykes, J., and T. Warnes. 1997. *I Don't Want to Take a Bath*. New York: Scholastic.

Taylor, M. 1997. *Roll of Thunder, Hear My Cry*. New York: Puffin.

Van Allsburg, Chris. 1985. *The Polar Express*. New York: Clarion.

———. 1986. *The Stranger*. New York: Clarion.

———. 1992. *The Widow's Broom*. New York: Clarion.

Wood, A., and D. Wood. 1984. *The Napping House*. New York: Harcourt Brace Jovanovich.

Wood-Brady, E. 1993. *Toliver's Secret*. New York: Random House.

PROFESSIONAL REFERENCES

Research is designated with an asterisk (*)

*Anderson, R. C., E. H. Hiebert, J. A. Scott, and I. A. G. Wilkinson. 1985. *Becoming a Nation of Readers*. Washington, DC: U.S. Department of Education.

Baldwin, C. 1994. *Calling the Circle: The First and Future Culture*. Newberg, OR: Swan Raven.

*Beck, I. L., M. McKeown, R. Hamilton, and L. Kucan. 1997. *Questioning the Author: An Approach to Enhancing Student Engagement with Text*. Newark, DE: International Reading Association.

Buber, M. 1958. *I and Thou*. Trans. R. G. Smith. New York: Macmillan.

Burns, M. S., P. Griffin, and C. E. Snow, eds. 1999. *Starting Out Right: A Guide to Promoting Children's Reading Success*. Washington, DC: National Academy Press.

Cahill, S., and J. Halpern. 1992. *Ceremonial Circle*. San Francisco: HarperCollins.

Cole, A. 2001. *Better Answers: Written Performance That Looks Good and Sounds Smart*. Portland, ME: Stenhouse.

Costa, A. L., and R. J. Garmston. 1994. *Cognitive Coaching: A Foundation for Renaissance Schools*. Norwood, MA: Christopher-Gordon Publishers.

*Csikszentmihalyi, M. 1990. *Flow: The Psychology of Optimal Experience*. New York: HarperCollins.

*Cunningham, P. M., and R. L. Allington. 1994. *Classrooms That Work: They Can ALL Read and Write*. New York: HarperCollins College Publishers.

*DeCecco, J., and A. Richards. 1974. *Growing Pains: Uses of School Conflict*. New York: Aberdeen Press.

*Deutsch, M. 1973. *The Resolution of Conflict*. New Haven, CT: Yale University Press.

Dewey, J. 1949. *Knowing and the Known*. Westport, CT: Greenwood Press.

*D'Aluisio, F., and P. Menzel. 1996. *Women in the Material World*. San Francisco: Sierra Club Books.

*Etzioni, Amitai. 1993. *The Spirit of Community: The Reinvention of American Society*. New York: Simon & Schuster.

Gawain, S. 1993. *The Path of Transformation*. Novato, CA: Nataraj Publishing.

Griffin, J. 2001. *How to Say It from the Heart*. Paramus, NJ: Prentice-Hall.

Harris, A. J., and E. R. Sipay. 1985. *How to Increase Reading Ability*. New York: Longman.

Harvey, S., and A. Goudvis. 2000. *Strategies That Work: Teaching Comprehension to Enhance Understanding*. York, ME: Stenhouse.

*Heath, S. B. 1983. *Ways with Words*. New York: Cambridge University Press.

Holland, G. B. 1998. *A Call for Connection: Solutions for Creating a Whole New Culture*. Novato, CA: New World Library.

International Reading Association and the National Council of Teachers of English. 1996. *Standards for the English Language Arts*. Newark, DE: IRA and NCTE.

Jacobsohn, R. W. 1998. *The Reading Group Handbook: Everything You Need to Know to Start Your Own Book Club*. New York: Hyperion.

Joe Gould's Secret. 2000. Directed by Stanley Tucci. October Films.

*Johnson, D. W., and R. T. Johnson. 1995. *Reducing School Violence Through Conflict Resolution*. Alexandria, VA: Association for Supervision and Curriculum Development.

*Johnson, R., D. Johnson, and E. J. Holubec. 1990. *Circles of Learning*. Edina, MN: Interactive Books.

*Keene, E. O., and S. Zimmerman. 1997. *Mosaic of Thought: Teaching Comprehension in a Reader's Workshop*. Portsmouth, NH: Heinemann.

Kohn, A. 1996. *Beyond Discipline: From Compliance to Community*. Alexandria, VA: Association for Supervision and Curriculum Development.

Maclean, P. D. 1995. *The Triune Brain*. New York: Plenum.

Manzo, K. 2002. "Students Polishing Their 'Table' Talk." *Education Week*, 5 June.

*Mehan, H. 1979. *Learning Lessons: Social Organization in the Classroom*. Cambridge, MA: Harvard University Press.

Miller, S. M., and S. Legge. 1999. "Supporting Possible Worlds: Transforming Literature Teaching and Learning Through Conversations in the Narrative Mode." *Research in the Teaching of English* 34 (1): 10–64.

Morgan, A. 1993. "Homo Sapiens: The Community Animal." In *In the Company of Others*, ed. C. Whitmyer. New York: Perigee.

New York State Education Department. 1999. *Primary Literacy Profiles*. Albany: State University of New York Education Department.

Peck, M. S. 1987. *The Different Drum: Community Making and Peace*. New York: Simon & Schuster.

Phillips Exeter Academy. 2002. "The Harkness Table." Accessed online at *<www.exeter.edu/pages/aca_harknesstable.html>*.

*Pressley, M. 2000. "What Should Comprehension Instruction Be the Instruction Of?" In *Handbook of Reading Research*, Vol. 3, ed. M. L. Kamil, P. B. Mosenthal, P. D. Pearson, and R. Barr, 545–562. Mahwah, NJ: Lawrence Erlbaum Associates.

*Public Broadcasting System. 1995. *The Human Language Evolves: With and Without Words*.

Sandra, J. N., J. Spayde, and the editors of *Utne*. 2001. *Salons: The Joy of Conversation*. Gabriela Island, BC: New Society Publishers.

*Schaps, E., Schaeffer, E., and S. McDonnell. 2001. "What's Right and Wrong in Character Education Today." *Education Week* 21 (2): 40, 44.

Smith, F. 1983. *Essays into Literacy*. Portsmouth, NH: Heinemann.

*Tannen, D. 1990. *You Just Don't Understand*. New York: Ballantine Books.

Walljasper, J., ed. 2002. "The Power of Talk." *Utne Reader* (July/August): 54.

Weaver, C. 1988. *Reading Process and Practice*. Portsmouth, NH: Heinemann.

Wheatley, M. 2002. *Turning to One Another: Simple Conversations to Restore Hope to the Future*. San Francisco: Berrett-Koehler.